Renewable Energy Law in Europe

Veröffentlichungen des Instituts für Energie- und Regulierungsrecht Berlin

Herausgegeben von Franz Jürgen Säcker

Band 50

PL ACADEMIC RESEARCH

Franz Jürgen Säcker/Lydia Scholz/Thea Sveen (eds.)

Renewable Energy Law in Europe

Challenges and Perspectives

PL ACADEMIC RESEARCH

Bibliographic Information published by the Deutsche Nationalbibliothek
The Deutsche Nationalbibliothek lists this publication in the Deutsche Nationalbibliografie; detailed bibliographic data is available in the internet at http://dnb.d-nb.de.

Library of Congress Cataloging-in-Publication Data
Renewable energy law in Europe : challenges and perspectives / Franz Jürgen Säcker, Lydia Scholz, Thea Sveen (eds.).
pages cm. – (Veröffentlichungen des Instituts für Energie- und Regulierungsrecht Berlin ; Band 50)
ISBN 978-3-631-66343-1
1. Renewable energy sources–Law and legislation–European Union countries.–Congresses. I. Säcker, Franz-Jürgen, 1941- editor. II. Scholz, Lydia, editor. III. Sveen, Thea, 1987- editor.
KJE6859.R46R46 2015
343.2409'2–dc23
2015028821

ISSN 2363-684X
ISBN 978-3-631-66343-1 (Print)
E-ISBN 978-3-653-05668-6 (E-Book)
DOI 10.3726/978-3-653-05668-6

PL Academic Research is an Imprint of Peter Lang GmbH.

Peter Lang – Frankfurt am Main · Bern · Bruxelles · New York · Oxford · Warszawa · Wien

This publication has been peer reviewed.

www.peterlang.com

Preface

It is the European Union's goal to establish a secure, sustainable and competitive supply of electricity. This is one of the fundamental objectives of its energy policy, and since the coming into force of the Lisbon Treaty firmly established in Article 194(1) TFEU. The goal has repeatedly been utilised by the European Commission, e.g. in the "Energy 2020" strategy and in the "Energy Roadmap 2050".

Since 1 January 2013, the objective of a common European market for energy is mandatory for EU Member States as well as for the states of the European Economic Area. An inherent part of such a common market and of European energy policy in general is the "triangle of objectives", namely environmental protection, security of supply and competitiveness, within which the EU's energy policy operates. It is binding for the legislative bodies of both, the EU and the Member States.

Pursuing all three objectives at the same time, each with maximum intensity, must lead to inconsistencies. As such, renewable energy renders the European energy supply more environmentally friendly, however, it still requires some form of promotion, which is in conflict with the market goal. According to the Renewables Directive, Member States are obliged to implement some kind of promotion scheme. There is, however, no permission to draft these schemes freely. Instead, promotion schemes have to be structured in such a way that they do not infringe upon provisions of the TFEU. In particular, a conflict with the principle of free movement of goods can arise when Member States limit their schemes' scope of application to plants on their own sovereign territory, thereby excluding electricity produced in other Member States. Furthermore, a conflict with the EU's State aid law may arise, especially given the financial advantages to the respective beneficiaries.

The law of renewable energies has always been subject to change. Having provided a certain degree of legal certainty with its *PreussenElektra* ruling in 2001, the ECJ specified the limits on national support schemes with a new wave of judgments, namely those in the cases of *Vent de Colère*, *Essent* and *Ålands Vindkraft*, in 2013 and 2014. At the same time, the European Commission issued its Guidelines on State aid for environmental protection and energy. These and other important developments regarding renewable energies in the EU and the European Economic Area have motivated the Berlin Institute for Energy and Regulatory Law and the Scandinavian Institute for Maritime Law of the University of Oslo to bring together energy law experts from Great Britain, Norway, Finland and Germany in order to exchange their ideas and perspectives. The workshop took place on

12 September 2014 in Berlin, one day after the ECJ had confirmed its decision in *Ålands Vindkraft* with its *Essent* judgment. The result was an inspiring event that covered diverse topics ranging from the relationship between Article 192 and 194 TFEU to the efficient development of an Offshore-infrastructure in the North Sea.

The editors very much thank Professor *Matthias Schmidt-Preuß* from the University of Bonn for having moderated the workshop with such exceptional dedication. Questions concerning his in-depth analysis of the competence of the EU in the field of energy (Articles 192, 194 TFEU) can be addressed to sekretariat.schmidt-preuss@jura.uni-bonn.de.

This volume contains a selection of the contributions to the workshop and is supposed to inform about the conducted debates and to encourage further research. The publication is made with consent of the University of Oslo's own publication series MARIUS – Scandinavian Institute of Maritime Law where the papers are co-published.

Berlin, June 2015
Franz Jürgen Säcker

Table of Content

Abbreviations

AG	Advocate General
BGBl.	Bundesgesetzblatt (Federal Law Gazette)
BerlKommEnR	Säcker (ed.), Berliner Kommentar zum Energierecht
CJEU	Court of Justice of the European Union
ch., chs.	chapter, chapters
CHP	combined heat and power production
CMLRev	Common Market Law Review (journal)
CO_2	Carbon Dioxide
COM	Communication of the European Commission
EC	European Community
EC Treaty	Treaty establishing the European Community
ECB	European Central Bank
ECJ	European Court of Justice
ECLR	European Competition Law Review (journal)
ECR	European Court Reports
ed., eds.	editor/edition, editors
EEA	European Economic Area
EEAG	European Commission, Guidelines on State aid for environmental protection and energy 2014–2020, 28.6.2014, OJ C 200/01
EEC	European Economic Community
EEC Treaty	Treaty establishing the European Economic Community
EEG	Erneuerbare-Energien-Gesetz vom 21. Juli 2014 (BGBl. I S. 1066), das zuletzt durch Artikel 1 des Gesetzes vom 29. Juni 2015 (BGBl. I S. 1010) geändert worden ist (German Renewables Act)
e.g.	exemplī grātiā (for example)
Electricity Market Directive	Directive 2009/72/EC of the European Parliament and of the Council of 13 July 2009 concerning common rules for the internal market in electricity and repealing Directive 2003/54/EC, OJ L 211/55
ELRev	European Law Review (journal)
esp.	especially

EStAL	European State Aid Law Quarterly (journal)
et al.	et alii
etc.	et cetera
EU	European Union
EuZW	Europäische Zeitschrift für Wirtschaftsrecht (journal)
f., ff.	folio, foliis (and following)
FIT	Feed-in Tariff
fn.	footnote
Gas Market Directive	Directive 2009/73/EC of the European Parliament and of the Council of 13 July 2009 concerning common rules for the internal market in natural gas and repealing Directive 2003/55/EC, OJ L 211/94
ibid.	ibidem (in the same place)
ICSID	International Centre for Settlement of Investment Dispute
i.e.	id est (that is to say)
LNG	non-liquified gas
no.	number
MW	Megawatt
NWV Neuer Wiss. Verl.	Neuer Wissenschaftlicher Verlag
NZKart	Neue Zeitschrift für Kartellrecht
OGEL	Oil, Gas & Energy Law
OJ	Official Journal
OUP	Oxford University Press
p.	page, pages
P. Lang	Peter Lang (publisher)
para., paras.	paragraph, paragraphs
RdE	Recht der Energiewirtschaft (journal)
Regulation on Cross-Border Trade for Electricity	Regulation 2009/714 of the European Parliament and of the Council of 13 July 2009 on the conditions for access to the network for cross-border exchanges in electricity and repealing Regulation (EC) No 1228/2003, OJ L 211/15
RES	Renewable Energy Sources

RES Directive	Directive 2009/28/EC of the European Parliament and of the Council of 23 April 2009 on the promotion of the use of energy from renewable sources and amending and subsequently repealing Directives 2001/77/EC and 2003/30/EC, OJ L 140/16
revsd.	revised
StrEG	Gesetz über die Einspeisung von Strom aus erneuerbaren Energien in das öffentliche Netz (Stromeinspeisungsgesetz) vom 7. Dezember 1990 in der Fassung vom 1. August 1994 (German Act on the promotion of renewable energies, now replaced by the EEG)
SWD	Staff Working Document
TEU	Treaty on the European Union
TFEU	Treaty on the Functioning of the European Union
TSO	Transmission System Operator
UK	United Kingdom
Utilities LRev	Utilities Law Review (journal)
WTO	World Trade Organisation
ZWeR	Zeitschrift für Wettbewerbsrecht (journal)

Introduction

The future framework for the promotion of renewable energies was the main topic for the in-depth legal discussion between the scholars and experts in the field of EU law present at the jointly organised seminar on 12 September 2014. The research seminar in Berlin was organised by the University of Oslo, Scandinavian Institute for Maritime law with UiO Energy and the Institute for Energy and Regulatory Law (Enreg) in Berlin. It provided an overview of the impact on the current developments in EU law within the sphere of renewable energy as well as a platform for discussion. This publication therefore comprises a selection of seminar papers written on the basis of the presentations held.

The triangular aim of European Union energy policy, notably achieving a functioning internal electricity market, promoting electricity generation from renewable energy sources and ensuring a high degree of security of energy supply faces several challenges. The European Commission has emphasised the significance of the aforementioned objectives in two communications which address both the completion of the internal energy market and the promotion of renewable energies.[1] At the heart of these aims figure renewable energy promotion, aimed at addressing all these three objectives at once. Thus, the EU and its Member States have implemented and continue to implement various measures addressing all these aims simultaneously. The objectives have been encapsulated into the energy provision, Article 194 TFEU, as an integral part of EU primary and further substantiated by secondary legislation such as the Electricity Market Directive, the Regulation on Cross-Border Trade for Electricity and the RES Directive. In addition, the Energy Strategy 2020[2], the Energy Roadmap 2050[3] and lastly the 2030 Framework[4] have been incorporated into the overall legal debate.

More than one decade has passed since the CJEU confirmed the conformity of the national scope of promotion schemes for renewable energies based on private

1 European Commission, Making the internal energy market work, 15.11.2012, COM(2012) 663 final and European Commission, Renewable energy: a major player in the European energy market, 6.6.2012, COM(2012) 271 final.

2 European Commission, An energy policy for Europe, 10.1.2007, COM(2007) 1 final.

3 European Commission, Energy Roadmap 2050, 15.12.2011, COM(2011) 885 final.

4 European Council Conclusions, 24.10.2014, EUCO 169/14.

payments.[5] Since the rendering of the *PreussenElektra* judgment[6], promotion and use of renewable energies have increased within a stronger European internal electricity market context. This evolution has indeed strengthened policies and legal measures promoting the use of renewable energies but also their potential conflict with the cardinal principle of free movement of goods as well as State aid rules. In light of this evolution, current developments of European Union case law will be closely examined.

National promotion schemes are still limited to the relevant national territory where the producers of the electricity operate. Member States still use feed-in schemes where renewable energy is promoted by private payments which are subject to control mechanisms governed by the State. Both situations have led to a new series of case law dealing with the compliance of national promotion schemes with the State aid rules and the free movement principles. The recently published Guidelines on State aid for environment and energy (EEAG)[7] have also fuelled the discussion. These new developments within the European legal and political landscape are deemed to have an impact on the way in which renewable energy in the EU and in the EEA could and should be promoted.

The first topic in this volume raises a general debate regarding the new environmental and energy State aid guidelines as well as the notion of State aid with regards to renewable energy promotion. As the enforcer of EU State aid rules, the European Commission plays an increasingly active role. Although the new guidelines are drafted as soft-law which is not *per se* binding within the *aquis communautaire*, the European Commission's discretion is bound by these guidelines and their nature is argued to be *quasi legislative*.[8] Further, Article 107(1) TFEU defines State aid as any selective advantage granted by a Member State or through State resources in any form whatsoever which distorts or threatens to distort competition, in so far as it affects trade between Member States. Articles 30 and 110 TFEU include product related provisions that are *legi speciali* to the fundamental freedom in Article 34 TFEU.[9] They have been neglected for a fairly long time; the

5 In order to facilitate the abbreviation used in the various contributions within this volume, the Court of Justice of the European Union will be referred to as the CJEU.

6 C-379/98 *PreussenElektra* [2001] ECR 2099.

7 European Commission, Guidelines on State aid for environmental protection and energy 2014–2020, 28.6.2014, OJ C 200/01.

8 This argumentation has been put forward by A. Johnston in his contribution to this volume. For detailed analysis, see A. Johnston, section IV 2 a).

9 C-74/76 *Iannelli & Volpi/Meroni* [1977] ECR 557, para. 9.

judgment in *PreussenElektra*[10] and the following legal debate have dwarfed those fiscal provisions. Thus, Articles 30 and 110 TFEU are relevant in the State aid assessment of national schemes to promote renewable energies.

The second topic in this volumes underlines that national legislative freedom in the field of renewable energies is not only limited by the State aid rules but also by the principle of free movement. With regards to the principle of free movement of goods, national promotion schemes have now three times challenged the CJEU to assess their compatibility with Article 34 TFEU and to further clarify the scope of the exemptions. Whereas the CJEU clearly confirmed the compatibility of the promotion schemes despite their discriminatory character in *PreussenElektra*[11], *Ålands Vindkraft*[12] and *Essent*[13], the impact of this series of case-law on the general free movement of goods conceptualisation has not been clarified. The new structure in general and the scope of the non-exhaustive *Cassis-list* of mandatory requirements in particular will therefore be critically discussed. The *Essent* judgment furthermore sheds light on the Court's current approach to Article 345 TFEU and the system of property ownership as well as on restrictions on capital movement and possible justifications. The multiple elements presented in the case mean that it has further implications both for the energy sector and more generally in relation to capital movement.

A third topic in this volume concerns investments and disputes. Investments are crucial to European renewable energy promotion but they also trigger remarkable disputes, litigation at many levels as well as limitations for the implementation of national promotion schemes. Renewable energy disputes are strikingly different from other energy disputes within Europe and internationally due to their scale. Although heavily regulated, it is the scale of renewable energy promotion in Europe that differentiates the investments as they all depend on the national subsidies schemes. These schemes in turn have a direct impact on the investments and regulatory frameworks.

The fourth topic covered in this volume provides a deeper understanding of the EU competences in the field of energy with the introduction of Article 194 TFEU in light of a predominant environmental purpose of renewable energy promotion. The boundary between energy security and environmental protection is certainly not clear from a legal perspective and this may enhance the risks of misinterpretations regarding the purpose and spirit of primary and secondary legislation at

---

10 C-379/98 *PreussenElektra* [2001] ECR, I-2099.

11 C-379/98 *PreussenElektra* [2001] ECR 2001, I-2099.

12 C-573/12 *Ålands Vindkraft*, not yet reported.

13 C-204/12 – 208/12 *Essent Belgium*, not yet reported.

the national level. The functioning and scope of the competences allocated to the EU as well as measures falling within the energy and environmental domain simultaneously raise several legal questions.

The seminar also addressed the legal questions deriving from the technical impacts of an increasing expansion of renewable energies. Due to the fact that electricity is grid dependent and that the use of volatile intermittent energies such as wind challenges the existing grid infrastructure, an effective congestion management accompanied by incentives to build new infrastructure is required. With respect to the electricity generation in offshore wind-farms, the idea of an integrated offshore grid infrastructure is discussed at European level. Although technical and economic assessments give evidence for the effectiveness for such a long-term and large-scale project, a series of legal questions arises on how to efficiently develop, operate and regulate an integrated grid which is subject to several national legal orders.

Lydia Scholz
Thea Sveen

Angus Johnston
Professor of Law, University College and Faculty of Law, University of Oxford
angus.johnston@law.ox.ac.uk

The impact of the new EU Commission guidelines on State aid for environmental protection and energy on the promotion of renewable energies

Content

I. Introduction

Energy and Environmental subsidies are clearly of great political and practical significance. Their importance is keenly felt at national and EU levels in terms of national policy-making and regulatory autonomy, allowing experiments to be conducted in different Member States how best to encourage renewables development and deployment. At the same time, external and independent scrutiny of such national subsidies can, in the long run, also be useful and important in helping to clarify the goals pursued by such schemes, including highlighting where some of those goals might be inconsistent *inter se* or with other important policy priorities (such as addressing energy price levels and their impact upon energy poverty, e.g.). Systems of subsidies are also of great significance for the position of numerous businesses: they may be encouraged to locate themselves in countries/regions where such financial or other support is available, but if they operate in energy-intensive industries then some energy subsidies may add further to their input costs, thus forcing up prices for final customers. Which, of course, makes clear that the availability of such subsidies has not inconsiderable implications for the positions of consumers – both of energy itself and of products and services requiring significant energy inputs in their creation/production.

Here, we are concerned with the *EU law* implications of such subsidies, in the context of renewable energy and the application of the EU's State aid rules.[1] At the core of the State aid provisions is Article 107(1) TFEU, which provides that:

> *Save as otherwise provided in the Treaties, any aid granted by a Member State or through State resources in any form whatsoever which distorts or threatens to distort competition by favouring certain undertakings or the production of certain goods shall, in so far as it affects trade between Member States, be incompatible with the internal market.*

II. Legal Structural Considerations

It is worth highlighting the reason to include institutional and structural material at the outset of the analysis. This is primarily because the rules and policies which are developed under EU law to address the free movement of, and State aid for,

1 The free movement rules – in particular the free movement of goods under Articles 34 and 36 TFEU – have also generated recent controversy in the renewables field. This issue is noted briefly below (section III 2), and is analysed in depth elsewhere in this volume: see in particular Scholz' comments on the reconstruction of the principle of free movements of goods (*Scholz*, section V), Penttinen (*Penttinen*, section III 3) and Steffens (*Steffens*, section II 4).

renewables will ultimately need to be applied and enforced by such institutions, with an understanding of their broader EU law context. The fact that, for example, many elements of EU free movement and State aid law rely upon national courts for their enforcement makes it important that EU-level case law, legislation and guidelines be clear, comprehensible and capable of application by national courts (and, indeed, national governments and authorities when seeking to design aid schemes and grant aid to renewables in individual cases). The interactions between these institutions, and the scope of their respective roles, are thus vital to understanding and developing EU free movement and State aid law in general, and in the renewables sector in particular.

1. Treaty bases

First, we must briefly consider on what authority the EU in general, and its various institutions in particular, may seek to act in addressing issues concerning renewable energy.

a) State aid: Articles 107 and 108 TFEU

These core elements of EU State aid law are located at the 'primary' (what one might for the EU view as the 'Constitutional') legal level:[2] the implications of this should not be forgotten when it comes to the application of these EU law rules in the Member States by their administrations and courts, and indeed by private parties. Given that the key element of State aid law – the prohibition on granting new aids without notification and approval[3] – has been found to be directly effective, coupled

2 In that Treaty rules are hierarchically superior to secondary legislation adopted thereunder, etc. See the judgment in Cases C-402 and 415–05 P *Kadi & Al Barakaat* [2008] ECR I-6351, and the analysis of AG Bot in Case C-573/12 *Ålands Vindkraft*, not yet reported, concerning the validity of certain elements of the second RES Directive in the face of Article 34 TFEU: this case is discussed further in section III 2 c, below. On 'constitutional' principles and hierarchy more generally, see: *Dougan*, When worlds collide! Competing visions of the relationship between direct effect and supremacy (2007) 44 *CMLRev* 931 and *von Bogdandy/Bast* (eds.), Principles of European Constitutional Law (Oxford: Hart Publishing, 2nd revsd. edn., 2011).

3 Article 108(3) TFEU, Case 120/73 *Lorenz* v. *Germany* [1973] ECR 1471.

with the supremacy of EU law[4] they can have far-reaching implications[5] where its strictures are not respected at national level. National courts must make appropriate remedies available under national law to secure recovery of such unlawfully implemented aid,[6] as well as making available a declaration that such aid must not be implemented and interim relief[7] against such implementation.

b) *Legal bases for EU legislative action on energy and environment: Articles 192 (Environment) and 194 (Energy) TFEU*

While the EU has had specific competence in the environmental field since the Single European Act of 1986, the advent of an explicit energy competence took place only when the Treaty of Lisbon entered into force in late 2009. This is not the place to offer a detailed examination of the scope of the EU's competence under Articles 192 (environment) and 194 (energy) TFEU.[8] Here, suffice it to note that potential difficulties may be raised due to uncertainties concerning the scope, and limitations upon the exercise of, the EU's legislative competence in the relevant fields of energy and the environment.[9]

Furthermore, precisely how that legislative competence interacts with other areas of EU law (e.g. State aid)[10] is as yet not entirely clear: we will return to this question in section IV 4, below.

---

4 Case 6/64 *Costa* v. *ENEL* [1964] ECR 585, and its progeny.

5 Such as the obligation upon a Member State to recover unlawfully implemented aid: *Lorenz*, n. 3, above.

6 Case 301/87 *France* v. *Commission* (*Boussac*) [1990] ECR I-307.

7 See the Opinion of AG Tesauro in Case C-142/87 *Belgium* v. *Commission* (*Tubemeuse*) [1990] ECR I-959, para. 7.

8 For analysis, see (e.g.): *Hancher/Salerno*, Energy Policy After Lisbon in: Biondi et al (eds.), EU Law After Lisbon (OUP, 2012), ch. 18., esp. section V; *Johnston/van der Marel*, Ad Lucem? Interpreting the New EU Energy Provision, and in particular the Meaning of Article 194(2) TFEU' (2013) 22(5) ELRev 181; and *de Sadeleer*, EU Environmental Law and the Internal Market (OUP, 2014), ch. 3.

9 For further analysis on the distinction and similarities between environmental and energy provision of the Treaty, see Sveen in this publication (*Sveen*, section II).

10 But also Articles 114 (internal market), 171 and 172 (Trans-European Networks) TFEU.

2. Secondary and tertiary level instruments

a) Secondary legislation

On the primary legal bases above, the EU's legislative institutions may adopt secondary legislation empowering,[11] or delegating to,[12] the Commission.[13] Such legislation may also lay down procedures for the performance of the Commission's various scrutiny and enforcement functions, either directly adopted by the Council[14] and the European Parliament or by the Commission itself after a suitable legislative measure of delegation. Most regularly, that delegation allows the Commission itself, in the pursuit of its enforcement tasks, to adopt Block Exemption Regulations,[15] assisting in the process of the application of EU law rules at national level by governments, courts and private parties alike.

b) Soft law guidance (etc)

Such measures concern how the Commission intends to conduct its role and exercise its powers in its fields of competence.[16] The designation of these measures

---

11 E.g. in in State aids, on the basis of what is now Article 109 TFEU, the Council adopted Regulation 994/98/EC [1998] OJ L142/1 (indeed generally known as the 'enabling Regulation'), allowing the Commission to enact (most recently) the General Block Exemption Regulation 651/2014/EU [2014] OJ l187/1.

12 See Article 290 TFEU. An important example is provided by the various versions of the 'Comitology' procedure, most recently embodied in Regulation 182/2011/EU [2011] OJ L55/13; and there are numerous specific provisions in various directives giving the Commission a role in scrutiny (e.g. Article 4 of RES Directive concerning National Renewable Energy Action Plans), and/or enforcement (e.g. Directive 98/34/EC laying down a procedure for the provision of information in the field of technical standards and regulations [1998] OJ L 204/37, esp. Articles 8 and 9 thereof) thereunder, etc.

13 Or, perhaps, other institutions in some circumstances: e.g. the Court of Auditors, the Committee of the Regions.

14 E.g. in Competition Law, Council Regulation 1/2003/EC [2003] OJ L 1/1; and in State aids, Regulation 659/1999/EC [1999] OJ L 83/1.

15 There are various examples in Competition Law, including: the Verticals Regulation 330/2010/EU [2010] OJ L 102/1, and various more specific measures (on Motor Vehicles, Technology transfer, etc): for discussion, see *Rose/Bailey* (eds.), Bellamy & Child: European Union Law of Competition (OUP, 7th ed., 2013), chs. 7 (on verticals) and 9.6 (on technology transfer). In State aids, we have now had two iterations of a General Block Exemption Regulation: Regulations 800/2008/EC [2008] OJ L241/3 and 651/2014/EU (n. 10, above).

16 E.g. in Competition Law, the Commission's Access to the File Notice [2005] OJ C325/7. For general coverage, see *Senden*, Soft Law in European Community Law (Oxford: Hart

as "soft law" means that they are not *binding* upon Member States, individuals and courts;[17] but they can bind the Commission, via the doctrine of 'legitimate expectations'.[18] The *European Night Services* judgment[19] of what was then the Court of First Instance provides a useful illustration of the implications of this point. There, the Court of First Instance emphasised that "the mere fact that [the Commission's] threshold [, in its Notice,[20] for an agreement to have more than a *de minimis* effect upon competition] may be reached and even exceeded does not make it possible to conclude with certainty that an agreement is caught by [what is now Article 101(1) TFEU]." Thus, the CFI did not consider itself bound by the Commission's Notice, and the UK's Office of Fair Trading published guidance which made clear that it would "have regard" to the Commission's approach on this question, but would assess each case in its own context and not treat itself as bound by the Commission's own Statement concerning *de minimis* agreements.[21] But if the Commission's own representation of how it will apply its policy in a given case is clear and induces reliance upon it by a private party to that party's detriment, then it may generate a legitimate expectation enforceable against the Commission.

3. Institutional aspects and roles

a) Council & European Parliament as legislator

Under the principle of conferred powers (or attributed competences), the power to legislate only exists in the areas, under the procedures and in the hands of the institutions specified in the power-conferring Treaty provisions.[22] In most such areas, after the Treaty of Lisbon we have reached the position that the Council and the European Parliament operate as co-legislators; however, it must be emphasised that there are caveats to this position in various areas. Crucially for our purposes, such caveats exist in the fields of energy (Article 194(2) TFEU) and the

---

Publishing, 2004); and for recent treatment in a more particular context, see *Stefan*, Soft law in Court: Competition Law, State Aid and the Court of Justice of the European Union (Kluwer Law International, 2012).

17 Case 322/88 *Grimaldi* v. *Fonds des maladies professionaelles* [1989] ECR 4407.

18 E.g. Case 120/86 *Mulder* v. *Minister van Landbouw en Visserij* [1988] ECR 2321.

19 Joined Cases T-374, 375, 384 and 388/94 *European Night Services* v. *Commission* [1998] ECR II-3141.

20 Commission Notice on agreements of minor importance [2001] OJ C368/13 (22 December 2001).

21 *Agreements and concerted practices* (OFT 401, 2004), paras. 2.19 ff.

22 Article 5(1) and (2) TEU.

environment (Article 192(2) TFEU), where certain subject-matter triggers 'special procedures'. These can involve unanimity being required within the Council and merely the consultation of the European Parliament (e.g. Article 192(2) and Article 194(3) TFEU), but may also involve other restrictions (see the second sentence of Article 194(2) TFEU).[23]

b) Commission

The Commission performs various functions under the EU's Treaties. It may act as a secondary or delegated legislator, whether directly under Treaty provisions[24] or by virtue of primary legislation adopted by the Council, or Council and European Parliament.[25] Perhaps its primary role is as the so-called 'guardian of the Treaties', serving as an enforcer of EU law via the Article 258 TFEU procedure and more generally as a watchdog of the application of EU law and the impact of EU rules and policies.[26] Finally, the Commission may operate as a policy developer[27] and is the sole institution authorised to act as initiator of legislative proposals under the ordinary legislative procedure.[28]

---

23 For discussion of the implications of the wording of this provision, see *Johnston/van der Marel*, 'Ad Lucem?', fn. 8, above.

24 E.g. Article 106(3) TFEU concerning services of general economic interest, although it should be noted that political pressure has been brought to bear upon the Commission in the past when it has suggested the adoption of measures under this provision and its predecessors: the Council and/or the European Parliament may object that the subject matter needs full legislative consideration. For an example, see the evolution of what became the first Internal Energy Market Directives on electricity (96/92/EC [1997] OJ L27/20) and natural gas (98/30/EC [1998] OJ L204/1), which the Commission originally hoped to pursue under what was then Article 90(3) EEC: see the notes by: *Trepte* [1992] Utilities LRev 18; and *Hancher* [1992] Utilities LRev 133, [1993] Utilities LRev 79 and [1994] Utilities LRev 64 for discussion.

25 See fn. 10 and 11 above.

26 In general, see Article 249(2) TFEU, concerning the annual report on the activities of the Union; more specifically, the set-up of the Treaties and/or the secondary legislation has in various areas established this role for the Commission in Competition and State aid law: for more details, see section II 2 a), above, and the references cited therein.

27 Consultations, Green and White Papers, reports to the Council and/or the European Council on key policy areas and developments. Often, the Council and/or European Council will then call upon the Commission to bring forward legislative proposals on particular topics.

28 Under Article 289(1) TFEU, although certain other areas allow legislation to be adopted on the initiative of a group of Member States or the European Parliament, or on the recommendation of the ECB or CJEU (Article 289(4) TFEU).

c) *Court of Justice (including General Court)*

Obviously, the EU-level judiciary has a crucial role to play in EU law in general, and in the field of State aid and free movement as it relates to energy in particular. In exercising their respective jurisdiction to hear and determine actions and proceedings, the Court of Justice and the General Court will provide interpretation of Treaty rules (including Articles 34 and 36, and 107 and 108 TFEU, as well as the Charter of Fundamental Rights), the provisions of secondary legislation, and general principles of law (such as legitimate expectations, non-retroactivity, and the like).[29] In short, the Court of Justice of the EU (which encompasses the Court of Justice and the General Court) must "ensure that in the interpretation and application of the Treaties the law is observed" (Article 19(1) TEU).

In the area of our particular interest, the Court will be faced with some role in the enforcement of EU law, where ruling on Commission enforcement actions and attempts to impose penalties upon recalcitrant Member States under Articles 258 and 260 TFEU, respectively. The General Court will also be the primary destination for challenges brought against Commission decisions in the State aid field; and as we shall see below (sections III 1 and III 2), a fruitful source of cases in this area is those referred to the Court of Justice under the preliminary rulings procedure of Article 267 TFEU.[30] The latter category is made up of cases which come from national courts, affected by the directly effective[31] nature of EU law rules on the free movement of goods and some elements of State aid law.

d) *National courts and authorities*

As a result of the directly effective nature of Article 34 TFEU and of the prohibition on Member States implementing unlawful State aid, national authorities are affected *ex ante* by this obligation. This means that there is a standstill obligation, preventing the implementation of such aid until its notification to and approval by the Commission;[32] but it also means that any such unlawfully implemented

29 See, generally, *Tridimas*, The General Principles of EU Law (OUP, 2nd ed., 2007).

30 To take some energy-related examples, see: Case 379/98 *PreussenElektra* [2001] ECR I-2099, Case C-262/12, *Vent de Colère!*, judgment of 19 December 2013, discussed in section III 1, below.

31 *Ibid.*, although it should not be forgotten that the Article 267 TFEU procedure was itself was a key vehicle for the development of the very concepts of direct effect and the supremacy of EU law: see n. 2, above.

32 Article 108(3) TFEU.

aid should be recovered by the relevant national authorities.[33] In what follows, the ability of national courts and authorities to contribute grist to the EU judiciary's interpretive mill in the energy field will become clear: many of the trickiest cases have arisen as a result of Member State schemes being challenged in national courts as being contrary to directly effective rules under the EU Treaties. They have presented both national systems and the EU institutions with difficult questions, both in the cases themselves and in accommodating the reasoning and outcomes of those cases in future enforcement, law- and policy-making in the energy and environmental area.

III. Role of the Court of Justice of the EU

To gain a broader picture of the context within which the EEAG will operate, we must consider the CJEU's case law and the implications of those developments, definitely in the field of EU State aid law, but by no means *only* with regard to State aid law.

1. EU State aid law

The term "State aid" has not been defined in the Treaty, but it has been held to require:

(1) a competitive advantage;[34]
(2) selectively conferred upon one undertaking or group of undertakings;[35]
(3) by the State or through State resources;[36]

---

33 See: Article 14(1) of Regulation 659/1999/EC [1999] OJ L83/1, where a negative Commission decision shall require Member States to "take all necessary measures to recover the aid from the beneficiary … [unless] this would be contrary to a general principle of [EU] law"; and, most recently, Case C-527/12 *Commission* v. *Germany* (*Beria group*) (judgment of 11 September 2014), and the cases cited therein.

34 Case C-256/97 *Déménagements-Manutention Transport SA (DMT)* [1999] ECR I-3913: has "the recipient undertaking receive[d] an economic advantage which would not have obtained under normal market conditions"?

35 See, e.g., Joined Cases 67, 69 and 70/85 *Kwekerij Gebroeders Van der Kooy* v. *Commission* [1988] ECR 219. In the case of RES support schemes, selectivity is usually easy to show, since such schemes by definition and design treat those producing renewable energy differently from others in the energy sector.

36 See, e.g., Case 730/79 *Philip Morris Holland B.V.* v. *Commission* [1980] ECR 2671 and Cases 296 and 381/82 *Netherlands and Leeuwarder Papierwarenfabriek* v. *Commission* [1980] ECR 809.

(4) which distorts or threatens to distort competition;[37] and
(5) which affects trade between the Member States.[38]

A full discussion of all of these elements is obviously beyond the scope of the present paper. Here, to give some background to recent developments and the scope of national arrangements which the EEAG will cover, we will focus upon the third element above: whether the advantage has been conferred by the State or through State resources. On that score, the first thing to note is that – in spite of the apparently clear wording of Article 107(1) TFEU, the CJEU has concluded that these two alternatives are in fact cumulative requirements, so that the aid must both stem from State resources *and* be attributable to the State.[39]

a) *PreussenElektra*

This conclusion was first reached in *PreussenElektra*:[40] at the time of the litigation, the German *Stromeinspeisungsgesetz* laid down a system to ensure that energy produced from renewable sources could gain access to the grid and thus to the national market. In line with the policy to support renewable energy, all 'electricity supply undertakings which operate a general supply network' were obliged to purchase all of the renewable electricity[41] produced within their area of supply.[42] Furthermore, they had to pay a fixed minimum price for that electricity, calculated on the basis of the average nationwide sales price for electricity. Those prices were set at such a level as to provide, in effect, a subsidy to generators of renewable electricity. This aspect had aroused some concerns under State aid law

37 Favourable treatment granted to a given sector within the scope of general taxation will normally be regarded as an aid (Case 70/72 *Commission* v. *Germany* [1973] ECR 813) but may also be sometimes objectively justified as a response to market forces (Case 67/85 *Van der Kooy* [1988] ECR 219, although that justification was not established in the case itself).

38 See, e.g., Case 102/87 *France* v. *Commission* (*Brewery loan*) [1988] ECR 4067. This criterion is generally very easily found to be satisfied – indeed, such an effect is often assumed if the other criteria are met.

39 Case C-379/98 *PreussenElektra* [2001] ECR I-2099, paras. 58–62; and Case C-482/99 *France* v. *Commission (Stardust Marine)* [2002] ECR I-4397, para. 24.

40 Case C-379/98 *PreussenElektra* [2001] ECR I-2099. For discussion, see, *inter alia*: *Bronckers/van der Vlies*, The European Court's *PreussenElektra* judgment: Tensions between EU principles and national renewable energy initiatives' (2001) 22(10) ECLR 458; *Cruz/de la Torre*, A Note on *PreussenElektra* (2001) 26 ELRev 489.

41 From specified sources: water, wind, sun and biomass (para. 1 StrEG 1998).

42 Para. 2(1), StrEG 1998.

and the Commission had been keeping a close eye on these developments. Under the original incarnation of this law in 1990, price levels had been set at 90% of the average sales price for wind-generated electricity[43] and 75% for other sources (increased to 80% by an amendment passed in 1994).[44] Over time, the level of subsidy in real terms had risen as production levels and efficiency, particularly in the wind power sector, had increased. The Commission had expressed doubts that this situation was compatible with the State aids rules and had suggested changes to the calculation of the subsidies involved.[45] Changes wrought by the 1998 legislation[46] implementing Directive 96/92/EC provided for a new compensation mechanism for the distributor in cases of 'hardship'. Under the German rules, the cost of supporting the subsidy for renewable power generation was borne by the distribution and/or transmission system operators, which in turn passed these costs on to final consumers in their access (etc.) pricing.

The Court held, contrary to the submissions of the Commission, that this meant that any resources transferred to the renewable electricity producers ultimately came from consumers and, crucially, not from *State* resources, nor were they granted directly by the State. Thus, those transfers did not amount to illegal State aid under EU law. It should be pointed out that the CJEU's judgment in *PreussenElektra* has been subjected to criticism by a number of commentators, on the ground that the Court took far too narrow an approach to the interpretation of the notion of the benefit being conferred from 'State resources', leading to different treatment being given under State aid law to functionally interchangeable State measures (e.g. such feed-in tariffs compared with specific taxation) which redistribute private resources to support other undertakings.[47] As Heidenhain has argued:[48]

---

43 Para. 3(2), StrEG 1990 (BGBl. 1990 I, 633).

44 BGBl. 1994 I, 1618.

45 Letter to the German Government, 25 October 1996, following complaints by the electricity supply undertakings about the impact of the renewables purchasing obligation upon them.

46 *Gesetz zur Neuregelung des Energiewirtschaftsrechts* (Law reforming the Law on the Energy Supply Industry) (BGBl. 1998 I, 730).

47 See, e.g., *Bronckers/van der Vlies* (n. 39, above), at 460–465, and *Cruz/de la Torre* (n. 39), at 490–494.

48 *Heidenhain* (ed.), European State aid Law Handbook (C.H. Beck, 2010), at 39 (emphasis in the original), citing a long line of earlier case law including: *Van der Kooy* (n. 34, above), para. 13 ff.; and the later judgment in Case C-206/06 *Essent Netwerk Noord* [2008] ECR I-5497, para. 65 ff.

> If one follows the [Court]'s long-standing case law concerning the attribution of resources to the State, pursuant to which all resources of private or public institutions [over] the allocation of which the State can exercise a decisive influence are to be considered State resources, regardless of their source, then – contrary to the assumption of the [Court] – the *resources of private undertakings, to the extent the State disposes of them by virtue of legislation*, should also be viewed as *'State resources'*.

As a result of the reasoning of the Court in *PreussenElektra*, it appears that a distinction has to be made between the different ways of administering the relevant RES support scheme. The German Feed-In Tariff system was held not to be State aid, given that it was not the State allocating the money to the recipients but the German TSOs, which paid the tariffs and equalized their costs among themselves in the market.[49] The Belgian and (initially) the Swedish quota systems did not amount to State aid either, for similar reasons: there is no penalty payment where there has been a breach of the quota obligation, and there is nobody managing such payments. Rather, the certificates are there, but no allocation of costs takes place.[50]

b) *Vent de Colère!*

In light of the foregoing discussion, the outcome reached in the CJEU's *Vent de Colère!* judgment[51] can be seen as fairly orthodox in that context.[52] There, the Court found that State resources were involved, because "the funds at issue … were … under public control and there was [a] mechanism …, established and regulated by the Member State, for offsetting the additional costs arising from that obligation to purchase and through which the State offered those private operators the certain prospect that the additional costs would be covered in full",[53] unlike the situation in *PreussenElektra*. Under the French scheme,[54] the costs of renewables support were imposed upon electricity operators by public service requirements, and were to be offset by what they were allowed to charge

49 Case C-379/98 *PreussenElektra* [2001] ECR I-2099.

50 Compare Case N504/2000 *British Renewables Obligation I* [2002] OJ C30/15, where the fine for breach of the obligation goes into a fund which is then distributed among renewable electricity producers.

51 Case C-262/12, judgment of 19 December 2013.

52 It must be noted that, for others, the case amounts to an expansion of prior jurisprudence on taxation and State resources, when compared with cases like *Stardust Marine*, *Pearle*, etc. For discussion, see the contribution of Steffens in this volume, *Steffens*, section II 3 and II 3 b.

53 Case C-262/12, para. 36.

54 *Ibid.*, para. 22 ff.

final customers of electricity. This transfer of resources was to be effected via network usage tariffs levied by the network operator; the relevant proportion of those charges was then transferred to the *Caisse des dépôts et consignations* – a public law corporation –, which centralised them in a special account and then paid them out to the electricity operators which had incurred the costs in paying for renewable electricity at a supported price. Further, the French State stood behind that public law corporation, guaranteeing that the State would cover extra costs involved for electricity operators in the scheme if charges collected from customers were not sufficient. Taken together, this mechanism and the State's involvement in its management and operation sufficed to render the relevant funds a 'State resource' for the purposes of EU State aid law. Of course, we must acknowledge the practical implications of such rulings that a national support scheme *did* amount to State aid and thus should have been notified to the Commission for clearance. In extreme cases, the EU's State aid rules could require aid beneficiaries to return the unlawful aid received,[55] and the implications of the *Vent de Colère!* judgment in that regard remain (at the time of writing) potentially difficult and controversial. To ameliorate these problems, the French government had requested that the Court limit the temporal effects of its finding that the French system did amount to State aid, but – in line with its previous case law on the subject – the Court found[56] that: first, the government should have been aware of the prohibition on implementing *prima facie* aid under Article 108(3) TFEU;[57] and, second, the financial consequences for a Member State cannot, in themselves, justify such a temporal limitation.

c) *The* CIDEF *case*

It might seem odd to offer separate treatment in a section concerning State aid in the energy sector to a judgment of the CJEU which concerns a French association representing turkey breeders. But both the Opinion of Advocate General Wathelet and the judgment of the Court in the *CIDEF* case[58] may yet offer an important contribution to future assessment of national RES promotion schemes

55 See *Lorenz*, n. 3, above.

56 Case C-262/12, paras. 41 and 42.

57 Perhaps somewhat harshly on these facts, given that the precise implications of *PreussenElektra* in this relatively novel field were – and indeed probably are – still being worked out during the time-frame (2000–2008) within which the French had developed their renewables support scheme: see, further, nn. 58–60, below.

58 Case C-677/11 *Doux Élevage* v. *CIDEF* (judgment of 30 May 2013).

where subsidies are involved. CIDEF is a French organisation representing turkey breeders, which undertook activities in the fields of publicity, promotions, external relations, quality assurance and research, funded by what were originally voluntary contributions from all of its members in the turkey industry in France; a decision of the French authorities had made such contributions to CIDEF compulsory by law, and had extended this to cover all participants in the French turkey industry. The claimants asserted that this State involvement rendered the scheme contrary to EU State aid law. The CJEU held that Article 107 TFEU did not apply to these arrangements, because:

> 36. … the national authorities cannot actually use the resources resulting from the [contributions] to support certain undertakings. It is [CIDEF] that decides how to use those resources, which are entirely dedicated to pursuing objectives determined by that organisation. Likewise, those resources are not constantly under public control and are not available to State authorities ….
>
> 40. [Thus,] … the State was simply acting as a 'vehicle' in order to make the contributions introduced by [CIDEF] compulsory, for the purposes of pursuing the objectives established by [CIDEF].

So far, this seems obviously in line with what has been discussed above. However, what might be more significant is the details offered by both the Court and its Advocate General in explaining why this did not constitute State resources granted by the State. The Court emphasised that the French decision to enshrine these contributions in law was not "dependent upon the pursuit [by CIDEF] of political objectives which are specific, fixed and defined by the public authorities" (para. 39); Advocate General Wathelet, meanwhile, advised that "something more specific and precise than a mere indication of the general objectives to be pursued … [such as] a description of the specific measures or activities that must be carried out in order to achieve those objectives" was required before sufficient State involvement and control could be shown. So, where a Member State has clearly defined policy objectives which involve a system to secure subsidies for a given activity, and that State is seeking strong control over how such policy goals are to be pursued and met by undertakings in the private sector, the *CIDEF* judgment suggests that EU State aid law may require serious consideration. Where the broad lines of national energy policy in general, and that concerning renewables in particular, are drawn with ever greater precision and detail by national governments, they run the risk of crossing the line drawn in *CIDEF*.

This might foreshadow greater scrutiny of Member State policies and schemes (levies, payments, etc.) being exercised by the Commission under EU State aid law obligations in future. Indeed, it chimes in harmony with the Commission's approach to its decisional practice under State aid law where national renewables support schemes have been concerned. That practice has generally sought to narrow the scope given to Member States by *PreussenElektra*, thus maximising the degree of State aid control over such national schemes which could be exercised by the Commission. That decisional practice has focused on (*inter alia*): the extent of State/public ownership of TSOs and/or DSOs[59] (where the feed-in tariffs are financed through such entities); the role of the State in managing accounts or bodies through which consumer contributions (via levies, etc.) are paid to TSOs or DSOs as compensation for the costs involved in renewables promotion;[60] and the analysis of detailed elements of green certificate systems.[61] The crucial question in these decisions has been whether the funds were at any stage under the control of the State in some way, a point which was emphasised by AG Jacobs as critical in his Opinion in *PreussenElektra*[62] and which was at the heart of the CJEU's recent judgment in *CIDEF*, as discussed above.

Whether this approach has been followed in the Commission's July 2014 clearance decisions for the latest UK[63] and German[64] renewables support schemes remains to be seen, when the formal text of these decisions is made public. Some have been critical of the Commission's decisions in this area for various reasons, arguing that the situation which obtains under the latest German renewables support scheme are functionally indistinguishable from that which was given a clean

59 E.g., *inter alia*, Cases: NN27/2000 *German Feed-In Tariff* [2002] OJ C164/5; N342/2003 *Danish Feed-in Tariff for Wind II* [2005] OJ C250/9; N354/2008 *Danish Feed-in Tariffs for Wind III* [2009] OJ C143/6; and NN53/2005 *State aid to the Hungarian coal industry* [2007] OJ C90/10. And see Case C-206/06 *Essent Netwerk Noord* [2008] ECR I-5497, where the publicly-owned status of *Essent* was a crucial part of the reasoning which found that the funds generated by the public levy on customers, and used to compensate stranded costs, amounted to State aid. See, most recently and in a similar vein, the Opinion of AG Jääskinen and the judgment of the Court in Case C-262/12 *Vent De Colère!* (19 December 2013).

60 See, e.g., Cases N707 and 708/2002 *MEP Scheme* [2003] OJ C148/12; Case N317a/2006 *Austrian Feed-in Tariff I* [2006] OJ C221/8 and Case N446/2008 *Austrian Feed-in Tariff II* [2009] OJ C52/12; and Commission Decision 2007/580/EC on the State aid scheme implemented by Slovenia in the framework of its legislation on qualified energy producers, Case C7/2005 [2007] OJ L219/9.

61 See, e.g., *British Renewables Obligation I* (n. 49, above) and Case SA.33134 (2011/N) *Romanian Green Certificates* [2011] OJ C244/2.

62 Case C-379/98 (n. 39, above), paras. 164 to 167 of the Opinion.

63 Commission Press Release IP/14/866 (23 July 2014).

64 Commission Press Release IP/14/867 (23 July 2014).

bill of health in *PreussenElektra* itself.[65] Others[66] seem to see these recent decisions as more or less in line with that earlier Commission practice[67] and, indeed, one could argue that the CJEU's approach in both *Vent de Colère!* and the earlier *CIDEF* case provides some support for the Commission's line, at least as far as concerns classifying these national measures as State aid in need of notification and justification. And a link could also be made between these State aid rules and decisions, on the one hand, and the Commission's RES 2030 proposals (and the 'iterative' process of assessing and developing national and EU approaches to renewables) which they envisage, on the other, on which see below (section IV 3).

2. And not just State aid law: do not forget the free movement of goods!

National-level subsidies and support schemes can have other effects, e.g. by creating restrictions upon the free movement of goods (Article 34 TFEU): this was first acknowledged in an already very familiar case and has recently returned to the forefront of debate in the renewables sector. Only a brief outline will be offered here, since these cases will be treated in more detail elsewhere[68] in this volume.[69]

a) *PreussenElektra*

The well-known case of *PreussenElektra*[70] addressed this question, especially in the Opinion of Advocate General (AG) Jacobs: he made clear that the German system's combination of a purchase obligation imposed upon electricity operators and a supported price required to be paid to renewables generators amounted to a measure having equivalent effect to a quantitative restriction upon the free movement of goods and was thus, *prima facie*, an infringement of what is now Article 34 TFEU. AG Jacobs highlighted that this was a directly discriminatory national rule, because it favoured specifically only *national* renewables. This raised the problem that, traditionally, only the grounds listed in Article 36 TFEU could

---

65 See, e.g., *Sandberg et al.*, The creeping scope of State aid in relation to energy taxes and charges (2014) 4(3) European Energy Journal 42, 46–49.

66 E.g. *Nysten/Voß*, Feed-in tariffs under attack? International law & regulatory action on Feed-in Tariffs (2014) 4(3) European Energy Journal 21, at 28.

67 See n. 39, above.

68 For the present author's approach to the cases prior to *Ålands Vindkraft* and *Essent Belgium*, see *Johnston/Block*, EU Energy Law (OUP, 2012), ch. 11, para. 12.154 ff.

69 See Scholz regarding the justification of national promotion schemes, *Scholz*, section 4.

70 Case C-379/98, n. 39, above.

justify directly discriminatory (i.e. 'distinctly applicable', in the terms of *Cassis de Dijon*[71]) trade restrictions,[72] whereas the broader range of mandatory requirements (also stemming from *Cassis de Dijon*) could rescue 'indistinctly applicable' (i.e. indirectly or non-discriminatory) restrictions. Crucially, such mandatory requirements specifically already included environmental protection as a justification for such trade restrictions.[73] AG Jacobs criticised the confused case law on the subject and encouraged the Court to adopt a clearer approach, either by acknowledging that mandatory requirements could in principle apply across the full range of trade restrictions under Article 34 or else by expanding our understanding of the Article 36 ground of the protection of the life of human, plants and animals to encompass environmental protection goals.

The Court, meanwhile, rather fudged or ducked the issue in its judgment, holding rather cryptically that the German rules were "not incompatible" with Article 34 "in the current State of [EU] law concerning the electricity market".[74] It did so by various references to various sources and reasons which might in general justify trade restrictions on environmental grounds: international Conventions concerning greenhouse gas emissions, Article 11 TFEU's reference to integrating environmental protection into EU law- and policy-making, as well as the aforementioned mandatory requirement and the wording of Article 36.[75] But the Court made no attempt to characterise the *nature* of the restriction upon trade (whether directly discriminatory or otherwise), as its own previous case law would have seemed to require.

b) The second RES Directive[76]

Article 34 TFEU implications were crucial background to the evolution of the negotiations which led to the adoption of this Directive. This is not the place to revisit these developments in detail.[77] Suffice it to record here that a number of Member States were concerned that any possibility that EU law would provide for

71 Case 120/78 *Rewe Zentral* v. *Bundesmonopolverwaltung für Branntwein* [1979] ECR 649.

72 Case 113/80 *Commission* v. *Ireland* [1981] ECR 1625.

73 Case 302/86 *Commission* v. *Denmark* (*'Danish Bottles'*) [1988] ECR 4607, para. 9.

74 Case C-379/98, n. 39, above, para. 81.

75 *Ibid.*, paras. 74–76.

76 See n. 2, above.

77 For an analysis written in the midst of the negotiation process that led to the second RES Directive, see: *Johnston et al.*, The Proposed New EU Renewables Directive: Interpretation, Problems and Prospects (2008) 17(3) European Energy and Environmental Law Review 126, esp. 129–141.

cross-border trade in some form of renewable energy certificate (in the original proposal, for Guarantees of Origin (GOs)) would ultimately function as a Trojan horse: sneaking into national RES promotion schemes, undermining them with the need to justify their scope being limited solely to nationally-produced renewables in the face of EU free movement law and inexorably leading to a pan-EU fully harmonised regime for RES promotion. This was in light of the fact that the 'State of liberalisation of the electricity market' in the EU had developed significantly since *PreussenElektra*, so that there were fears that the Court might take a more intrusive approach to national renewables promotion schemes in general, and particularly so if EU legislation were seen to facilitate cross-border trade in electricity and the associated certificates (whether GOs or national green certificates).

c) The latest cases before the CJEU

These issues have recently re-surfaced in what might have been (but has probably turned out not be) rather acute form in two recent cases before the Court: *Essent Belgium*[78] and *Ålands Vindkraft*.[79] In each case, AG Bot adopted potentially far-reaching conclusions; but each time the Court took a less intrusive approach, which seems likely to leave the great majority of the elements of pre-existing national renewables support schemes intact, at least *vis-à-vis* Article 34 TFEU. This dashed the hopes of many that the Court would provide a clearer analytical framework for assessing such national renewables support schemes under the free movement rules, and the calls of some for greater EU law intervention in the operation of such national schemes so as to open up their operation to installations located in other EU Member States. A comprehensive analysis will not be offered here;[80] rather, a general outline will be provided, highlighting some key points of broader significance due to their potential interlinkage with State aid issues.

aa) Ålands Vindkraft

This case involved the attempt by the Åland islands – which are Finnish territory, albeit constitutionally autonomous and geographically located much nearer to Sweden; and whose electricity grid on the islands was connected only to the Swedish grid, not the Finnish – wind farm to participate in the Swedish renewables

78 Joined Cases C-204 to 208/12, not yet reported.

79 Case C-573/12, not yet reported.

80 Again, see Scholz in this volume, *Scholz*, section IV 2.

support scheme. The Swedes refused, because that scheme was restricted to *nationally* located renewables installations.

AG Bot advised[81] that this *would* be possible under the second RES Directive, given its protection for such nationally-restricted schemes under Article 3(3) of that Directive, which leaves it open to one Member State to decide whether they wish to support renewables generated in another, but does not *require* that they do so. But AG Bot went on to find that the relevant provisions in that Directive were *themselves* an unjustifiable trade restriction and thus contrary to Article 34 TFEU.[82] This analysis rested upon the hierarchically superior position of the Treaty rules on free movement of goods, to which any secondary legislation remained subject.[83] In AG Bot's analysis, the advent of fuller liberalisation of the EU electricity market and the introduction of a system requiring mutual recognition of guarantees of origin so as to facilitate cross-border trade meant that the reasoning in *PreussenElektra* could no longer stand; he proceeded to reject various other grounds of justification pleaded (by the defendant and various intervening Member State governments) in the case.[84]

In a Grand Chamber judgment, however, the Court rejected the most serious of AG Bot's conclusions: the Court acknowledged that the RES Directive did in principle allow such nationally-restricted schemes, but did not consider that it provided sufficient detail in its harmonisation to preclude examination of such schemes' compatibility with Article 34 TFEU.[85] The Court thus proceeded to assess possible justifications for such *prima facie* trade restrictions, failing to distinguish between directly discriminatory and other types of national rules, but simply asserting that "[a]ccording to settled case-law, national measure that are capable of hindering intra-[EU] trade may *inter alia* be justified by overriding requirements relating to protection of the environment ...".[86] This was followed by a rather extensive assessment (running to 37 paragraphs[87]) of the proportionality

81 Case C-573/12 *Ålands Vindkraft*, not yet reported, paras. 44–51 of his Opinion.

82 Although he did recommend deferring the effects of a judgment to this effect for a 24-month period, to allow the necessary amendments to be made to the RES Directive (*Ibid.*, paras. 112–121).

83 *Ibid.*, paras. 54–77.

84 *Ibid.*, paras. 79–111.

85 *Ibid.*, paras. 56–63 of the judgment.

86 *Ibid.*, para. 77 (and see paras. 78–82).

87 *Ibid.*, paras. 83–119. This encompassed both the restriction of the Swedish scheme to green electricity produced in Sweden alone (paras. 83–104) *and* the combination of

of the national scheme and the national market for such Green Certificates, before concluding that the Swedish scheme was not precluded by Article 34 TFEU.

bb) Essent Belgium

This case concerned the Flemish green certificates scheme, which limited the energy regulator (VREG) to accepting Green Certificates or Guarantees of Origin for the fulfilment of the relevant renewables obligation. While the Flemish scheme allowed the government to make provision for accepting Green Certificates or GOs from other regions of Belgium or other EU Member States, this had not been completed; so, when Essent Belgium attempted to surrender Green Certificates from not only Flanders but also Wallonia and the Brussels Capital region, *and* GOs from producers established in the Netherlands and Norway, the VREG found that Essent Belgium had not met its renewables obligation and fined it accordingly. The VREG was willing to accept GOs as if they were a national Green Certificate, but *only* if the GOs had been generated in Flanders (as per the Flemish rules) and not those which came from Wallonia or, indeed, from other Member States.

AG Bot – in his Opinion of 8 May 2013 (which thus preceded his Opinion in *Ålands Vindkraft*, above) – considered this to be an unjustifiable trade restriction. It created a *prima facie* trade barrier because domestic producers had the opportunity to sell Green Certificates to earn revenue over and above the price of electricity *and* because non-Flemish electricity suppliers would be discouraged from importing electricity into Flanders due to the need to purchase Flemish Green Certificates, given that their foreign GOs would not be accepted as fulfilling the renewables obligation imposed within Flanders.[88] AG Bot put in a plea for the Court to address the characterisation of such national measures as directly discriminatory, followed by the suggestion that it be expressly acknowledged by the Court that environmental protection goals are capable of justifying even directly discriminatory national trade-restricting measures, on the basis that EU law requires the EU to integrate (Article 11 TFEU) environmental protection objectives into its definition and implementation of EU policies.[89] AG Bot then analysed the various possible grounds of justification for such national restrictions and concluded that none applied here: in so doing, he stressed the need "to take into

---

that territorial restriction with other features of the scheme so as to offer a view of the operation of the system as a whole (paras. 105–119).

88 Joined Cases C-204 to 208/12 *Essent Belgium*, not yet reported, paras. 80–82 of the Opinion: a point acknowledged by the Court in its judgment (paras. 83–88), itself cross-referring to its judgment in *Ålands Vindkraft*, not yet reported, paras. 67–75.

89 *Ibid.*, paras. 92–97.

account the advantages that may arise from trade in green electricity within the European Union", arguing that "there is reason to believe that it might contribute to reducing the cost of renewable energy by permitting a more rational location of production".[90] The Court handed down its judgment on 11 September 2014 and, again, adopted a more lenient approach than its Advocate General towards the national scheme *vis-à-vis* Article 34 TFEU. It repeated much of its analysis from its *Ålands Vindkraft* judgment, and emphasised that any fine imposed for failure to meet the relevant national renewables obligation must not be excessive and should only go as far as is required to incentivise producers to increase renewables production and traders to take steps to acquire the requisite certificates.[91]

In both cases, the Court conducted a far more detailed scrutiny of the relevant national scheme under the proportionality heading than had been evident in *PreussenElektra*; at the same time, the justificatory framework thus provided ultimately falls to the national courts in these cases to apply to the facts of each case, although it is tolerably clear from the analysis of the Court in both cases that it should be relatively straightforward for the national courts to conclude that the justifications are made out in practice.

Another point which arose in both cases was the possibility that such national renewables promotion schemes could (or even should?) be opened up to participation from installations in other EU Member States: this was raised by the claimants in both cases and clearly was an argument which AG Bot found convincing in his Opinion in *Essent Belgium*. The Court was not persuaded, however, and instead emphasised that this question was one which needed to be answered when assessing the justifiability of the national schemes on the facts. In particular, provided that the domestic regimes offered a well-functioning market upon which local certificates could be purchased by importers or traders to accompany the electricity, this would render the national market sufficiently accessible for the territorial restriction with regard to such national certificates to be justifiable

---

90 *Ibid.*, para. 110. AG Bot also criticised the practice adopted by the VREG in its willingness, effectively, to transform a Flemish GO into a Green Certificate (*Ibid.*, paras. 112–113), which he argued could significantly disrupt the operation of Green Certificate systems, particularly given that GOs were explicitly to be treated separately – and perform a different function – from Green Certificates under national support schemes, both in the first Renewables Directive 2001/77 and its successor Directive 2009/28 (on which see, also, the judgment of the Court in *Essent Belgium*, para. 64, and AG Bot's Opinion in *Ålands Vindkraft*, not yet reported, paras. 46–51).

91 Joined Cases C-204 to 208/12 *Essent Belgium*, not yet reported, para. 114 of the judgment.

as part of the overall scheme.[92] It should be noted that this point does have potential implications beyond the renewables sphere. National capacity payments schemes (intended to safeguard electricity supply security) may raise similar issues concerning the free movement of goods between Member States, provided that interconnection capacity is sufficient for generators established in other Member States to make a genuine contribution to supply in times of shortage in the 'home' Member State. This matter is highlighted briefly below (section 4.2.2.2, *infra*).

IV. Role of the European Commission

1. Role under the Treaty and legislative framework

a) *Decision-maker and enforcer*

In the field of State aid law concerning the energy sector, the Commission performs a crucial function as decision-maker on notifications by Member States, and/or highlighting and pursuing failures to notify national aid schemes. Important examples are provided by various national RES(-E) promotion schemes notified to the Commission for State aid clearance: it is clear that the Commission has used its assessments of these schemes as a vehicle for limiting the impact of the Court's judgment in *PreussenElektra*, as discussed above (section III 1). And, of course, there has been a string of recent high profile recent cases concerning: the new German renewables regime;[93] the UK proposals for Contracts for Difference, especially for new nuclear at Hinkley Point C,[94] but also for renewables support.[95] Also concerning the UK, the Commission concluded that it would raise no objections to the UK's proposals for capacity mechanisms to secure generation adequacy.[96]

---

92 Case C-573/12 *Ålands Vindkraft*, not yet reported, paras. 113–118 of the judgment; joined Cases C-204 to 208/12 *Essent Belgium*, not yet reported, paras. 104–112 of the judgment.

93 'Commission approves German renewable energy law EEG 2014' (IP/14/867, 23 July 2014).

94 See: Commission, 'State Aid SA.34947 (2013/C) (ex 2013/N) – Investment Contract (early Contract for Difference) for the Hinkley Point C New Nuclear Power Station [2014] OJ C69/60 (7 March 2014). Recent news reports suggest that the scheme will be cleared by the Commission: 'Hinkley nuclear reactor project gains EU approval, leak reveals' (*The Guardian*, 22 September 2014).

95 'Commission authorises UK aid package for renewable electricity production' (IP/14/866, 23 July 2014).

96 See the Commission's Staff Working Document on Generation Adequacy in the internal electricity market – guidance on public interventions, SWD(2013) 438 (5 November 2013, available at: http://ec.europa.eu/energy/gas_electricity/doc/com_2013_public_

b) *Sole right of legislative initiative*

Under Article 289(1) TFEU, the Commission retains the sole right to make legislative proposals across most of the EU's fields of competence (where the ordinary legislative procedure applies), including energy, environment and the internal market. In the field presently under discussion, prominent examples are provided by the Commission's 2008 proposals for a second renewables directive,[97] and its 2014 proposal for changes to the EU's Emissions Trading System.[98] In the near future, further proposals on renewables and energy efficiency are to be expected, following on from the Commission's recent Communication on climate and energy in the 2020–2030 period.[99]

c) *Development of Guidelines, etc.*

Based upon past experience, information-gathering, decision-making practice, the Commission may adopt Guidelines, with a view to informing those subject to EU law requirements about how the Commission intends to perform its role of scrutiny, decision-making and enforcement:

Often, the creation of such Guidelines and their subsequent application can lead to formal legislation (e.g. Block Exemption Regulations under the Commission's delegated legislative powers; or a Decision on particular issues). The current State aid General Block Exemption Regulation 651/2014/EU develops and builds upon its 2008 predecessor, which itself evolved out of the Commission's development of Guidelines on various aspects of State aid law, which were themselves the result of the Commission's decisional practice. Once such provisions

---

intervention_swd01_en.pdf), and its subsequent announcement that it had authorised the UK's Capacity Market electricity generation scheme (IP/14/685, 23 July 2014). The formal document confirming that no objections would be raised was published on 17 September 2014: State aid SA.35980 (2014/N-2) – United Kingdom Electricity market reform – Capacity market, C (2014) 5083 final (23 July 2013, available at: http://ec.europa.eu/competition/State_aid/cases/253240/253240_1579271_165_2.pdf).

97 Commission, Proposal for a Directive of the European Parliament and of the Council on the promotion of the use of energy from renewable sources, COM(2008) 19 (23 January 2008).

98 Commission, Proposal for a Decision of the European Parliament and of the Council concerning the establishment and operation of a market stability reserve for the Union greenhouse gas emission trading scheme and amending Directive 2003/87/EC, COM(2014) 20 (22 January 2014).

99 Commission, Communication: A policy framework for climate and energy in the period from 2020 to 2030, COM(2014) 15 (22 January 2014).

are transformed into formal, binding legislation, their status changes, allowing Member State governments and private parties to rely upon them as directly applicable law, enforceable in national courts. This can affect their drafting style, but also has important impacts upon the relative institutional roles of the Commission, national courts and national authorities, in that a national aid scheme drafted in accordance with these rules need no longer be notified for approval. Instead, they receive an automatic, directly applicable exemption from the application of the *prima facie* prohibition in Article 107(1) TFEU.

But where such instrument remain as 'only' soft law Guidelines in form, then they function as indications of how the Commission will exercise its decision-making powers under the Treaty and/or secondary legislation. Insofar as clear representations of the Commission's approach are made, those affected by the Guidelines are entitled to rely upon them as generating a legitimate expectation as to how their situation will be handled by the Commission. In that sense, such Guidelines can serve to bind the Commission in its exercise of its functions under State aid law Nevertheless, the more detailed the drafting of such Guidelines, the greater their potential to act as *de facto* legislation in steering (or perhaps even forcing) Member States to take particular approaches in – here – their design of renewables support mechanisms. With this background in mind, we can move to examine the implications of the latest Guidelines issued by the Commission.

2. The 2014 Energy and Environmental Aid Guidelines (EEAG)

a) Core focus of the EEAG

The Commission's 2014 Energy and Environmental Aid Guidelines (EEAG), so far as renewable energy support schemes are concerned, are strongly focused upon the integration of renewables into the market: both in general, concerning the sale of electricity *per se*;[100] and with regard to competition *between* renewables technologies.[101] There is also at least an implicit concentration on the impact of such support schemes upon energy prices.[102]

All of this serves to underline the competition- and market-oriented approach that permeates the EEAG. A clear shift is observable in the text of the EEAG: at the outset, the Guidelines list numerous environmental goals and policies which

100 Para. 124.

101 Para. 126: general terms, and specific possible exception to limit to "specific technologies" later in the same paragraph; and on Green Certificate systems, see para. 137.

102 See para. 35 concerning affordability and para. 108's reference to "cost-effective delivery".

might be pursued by the grant of State aid.[103] Yet the wording and approach have shifted by the time the specific material concerning renewables support schemes arrives. Paragraphs 108 and 109 recount that the Commission expects renewables to be "grid-competitive" at some point between 2020 and 2030, and that the transition to cost-effective delivery should be made through market-based mechanisms and competitive bidding across the EEU from *all* RES on an equal footing. This market-based approach using competitive bidding becomes, at the very least, the default position in paragraph 109, and will apply *unless* "specific exceptions" can be justified on grounds of the size of the installation, some biofuels support or ETS-related questions (paragraphs 111 to 115). That this is the default approach is underlined by the Commission's presumption (paragraph 116) that national aid schemes which respect that approach will be appropriate and proportionate.

The result of this approach from the Commission brings with it clear(er) specification of *exceptions* from the general rule(s): e.g. so far as energy-intensive industries,[104] capacity mechanisms,[105] and small-scale generation[106] are concerned. But, overall, competitive tendering for renewables without technology differentiation[107] is presented as the main process,[108] a feed-in *premium*[109] – and *not* a feed-in tariff – or green certificates[110] are the 'appropriate' types of support instrument, due to their more market-oriented nature, and a measure of procedural streamlining is the prize on offer to Member States for using 'acceptable' approaches.[111]

---

103 Paras. 3 to 9.

104 Section 3.7, paras. 167–200 (tax reductions/exemptions; reduction in funding of RES support).

105 Section 3.9 on generation adequacy, paras. 216–233.

106 Para. 127.

107 Although it is acknowledged that there may be circumstances where tendering for specific technologies might be appropriate (para. 126), but this would need to be justified on grounds of: longer-term potential of a "new and innovative technology"; "diversification"; "network constraints and grid stability"; "system integration costs"; or avoiding "distortions on the raw materials markets from biomass support". Whether this amounts to a significant constraint upon Member State autonomy in designing national RES support mechanisms will depend upon how stringently the Commission intends to assess proof of such justifications for differentiation.

108 Paras. 109, 126.

109 Para. 124(a): because the electricity price is subject to market pressures and only the premium is set in advance (unlike in a feed-in tariff system, where the full tariff is set).

110 Paras. 135–137: because the certificate price is determined by market forces and is not determined in advance.

111 Para. 116.

b) Possible criticisms

As a preliminary point, one might question just how far the EEAG really build upon previous Commission experience in its decisional practice concerning Member State RES support schemes. After all, very few Member States to date have employed any version of a tendering or auction-based scheme in this area.[112] The main location where a clear shift over time has taken place towards an auction-based system has been under the EU ETS,[113] rather than in the renewables field. There is, however, experience of green certificate systems in national practice and Commission decisions, so this element of the EEAG rests on somewhat firmer foundations, at least so far as prior experience is concerned.

aa) Quasi-legislative nature of the EEAG? (Link to Article 194 TFEU)

The extent of prescriptive detail on various points throughout the EEAG raises the concern that the Commission has sought to use Guidelines as a vehicle for creating *de facto* legislation which serves to harmonise national renewables support mechanisms. Examples of this tendency in the EEAG are:

- the insistence upon using a feed-in premium rather than a feed-in tariff: while the EEAG do not expressly outlaw the use of tariff-based systems, so that a Member State could in principle notify such a system, the EEAG's drafting conveys the impression that the Commission would be highly unlikely ever to approve such a proposal;
- the requirement that aid beneficiaries be subjected to balancing responsibilities as a condition of approval of proposed aid; and
- the apparently limited scope for applying specific Member State approaches to the type of support scheme in general, and to technological differentiation in particular.

The quasi-legislative nature of the EEAG is strongly underlined by the inclusion of a requirement for Member States to bring existing aid 'into line' with the approved

---

112 For an outline, and more detailed discussion of a recent, small-scale auctioning process in Cyprus, see: Kylili/Fokaides, Competitive auction mechanisms for the promotion [of] renewable energy technologies: The case of the 50 MW photovoltaics projects in Cyprus (2015) 42 Ren. & Sust. Energy Reviews 226 (forthcoming, available online through http://www.journals.elsevier.com/renewable-and-sustainable-energy-reviews).

113 For recent discussion of the design of such systems in general, and coverage of the development of the EU's ETS, see *Weishaar*, Emissions Trading Design: A Critical Overview (Edward Elgar, 2014), 67–72 and ch. 5.

types of scheme: paragraph 126 envisages a transitional phase where competitive bidding should be introduced for at least 5% of all renewables capacity. Then, from 1 January 2017, all aid must be granted on the basis of a competitive bidding process: this is described as part of the "requirements" for aid to be cleared. Such language strikes a very legislative tone and seems to leave little room (subject to certain specific, seemingly narrowly defined exceptions) for Member State differentiation or experimentation. And this is all underlined by the incentive to toe the line, in the form of the various 'presumptions' as to the appropriateness and proportionality of a support scheme which the Commission declares that it will apply under EEAG if certain approved approaches are used by Member States (again, in para. 126).

This rather begs the question: is the adoption of such essentially legislative measures in the form of Guidelines, and solely under the Commission's (admitted) competence to administer the EU's State aid rules, really an appropriate use of the Commission's powers? One might query the compliance of the EEAG with important general principles of EU law such as subsidiarity and proportionality,[114] as well as whether the EEAG leaves sufficient room for the pursuit of those important environmental goals to which the Guidelines referred in its earliest paragraphs. Furthermore, the extent of harmonisation that may be created by such far-reaching and prescriptive Guidelines presents a significant challenge to the Member State's ability "to determine the conditions for exploiting its energy resources, its choice between different energy sources and the structure of its energy supply": these are "rights" vouchsafed to Member States under the second sentence of Article 194(2) TFEU, which they are entitled to protect (somehow: see, further, section 4.4, below) in the face of legislative measures adopted under the first sentence of Article 194(2) TFEU. Can the Commission simply by-pass this protection for Member States by proceeding solely upon the basis of its State aid powers and role? We will return to this point shortly.

bb) 'Forcing' the use of a feed-in premium (under tendering)

There has been much debate over the years concerning the most effective and efficient support mechanisms to pursue renewables development and deployment in the EU. It is thus highly noteworthy that the Commission's Guidelines on this subject seem determined to force Member States to adopt either green certificate systems or a feed-in premium via a competitive tendering process, and in the process to reject the use of feed-in tariffs. And this is in spite of the clear wording

114 See Article 5(3) (subsidiarity) and (4) (proportionality) TFEU.

of Article 2 of the Second RES Directive, which provides that "support schemes … shall include feed-in tariffs".

It might be speculated that the market integration goal was pushed strongly by DG Competition in the drafting, discussion and final text of the EEAG and anecdotal – but sadly not on-the-record – evidence suggests that this may have been the case. A desire to be seen to be taking action to try to reduce the costs imposed by national renewables support schemes upon the final customer's energy bill may also have played a role. Of course, in principle both of these objectives are laudable and consistent with the EU's general approach to energy market liberalisation, trade and competition. Yet one wonders whether the strictures of the new EEAG have left enough policy space for a sufficient focus upon actual Research, Development and Deployment (RD&D) of innovative renewable energy technologies. In particular, many economists fear that the EEAG will undermine financing conditions for capital-intensive technologies like wind and solar power, because under feed-in premium systems investors in such generation will need to find long-term contractual counter-parties to hedge against fluctuations in future wholesale power prices.[115] The only likely counter-parties would be the incumbent utilities, who would have neither strong incentives to offer favourable terms for such contracts, nor the need for the volume of renewable electricity that would be likely to meet renewables targets in the medium to long term.[116] This group of economists concluded their 'Open Letter' to the then relevant Commissioners Oettinger and Almunia as follows:

Market premiums risk the efficiency of short-term, and the effectiveness of forward contracting, markets and increase the costs of financing. They advantage incumbents, create barriers to new entrants, and raise the cost of meeting the renewable targets. They fail DG COMP's stated intention that aid for renewables should be at least cost to society. If the EU wants to achieve the policy objectives of advancing the EU energy market, reducing costs to consumers, and delivering the EU energy security, renewable and climate targets, it should allow for the option of using easier to manage feed-in systems.[117]

On one element of the EEAG, at least, there is a clear and strong link to the reasoning employed in the *Essent Belgium* and *Ålands Vindkraft* cases: this concerns

115 See the Open letter of European economists on market premiums to Commissioners Günther Oettinger and Joaquin Almunia (24 March 2014, text available at: http://www.renewablesinternational.net/negative-prices-from-priority-for-renewables/150/537/81835/).

116 *Ibid.*

117 *Ibid.*

the requirement that tenders for renewable energy supply must be open to generators in other Member States as well as in the Member State setting up the particular support scheme. The same point has also arisen clearly in the discussion and analysis of capacity mechanisms and measures to ensure generation adequacy (and the Commission Decision on the UK's proposed system for capacity payments[118]). It is evident from the reasoning of Advocate General Bot's Opinions in both of these cases[119] that such national schemes could be required to be open to 'foreign' generators in this way, and the approach taken by the Court of Justice[120] would seem to be similar, if somewhat more lenient in its willingness to accept that territorial restrictions (i.e. to allow the participation only of national generators in such schemes) could be justifiable under Article 34 TFEU.

3. Link(s) to the expected 2030 RES proposals?

The Commission clearly makes the connection[121] between assessing national RES support proposals under the EEAG on State aid grounds and the need to remember that such proposals are made in light of the need to meet the 2020 (and, in time, no doubt the 2030) renewables targets.[122] First, it is clear that there may be very positive synergies between future State aid assessment of Member States' proposals for RES support schemes and the application and development of EU law and policy on renewables. One key example concerns the acknowledgment that there will be significant challenges for cross-border co-operation and co-ordination in infrastructure and generation projects, if renewables are to develop and contribute to the energy mix as is hoped. If RES support is eligible for State aid clearance only provided that the national scheme is opened up to generators located in other Member States, this is likely to sharpen the focus of Member States and the Commission on issues of cross-border capacity, offshore connections and even grids, and the question of joint development by (actors from) different

118 See n. 95, above.

119 See the discussion of *Ålands Vindkraft* and *Essent Belgium* in section III 2, above.

120 *Ibid.*

121 See paras. 3, 5, 8, 9, 107 and 108.

122 Even if it now seems certain that these are to be non-binding in nature at national level. The impact upon generation adequacy of meeting such renewables targets also permeates the UK's Contract for Differences proposal concerning the Hinkley Point C new nuclear power station: see n. 93, above, at (e.g.) paras. 18 and 251.

Member States.[123] In this regard, the Commission's 'policy framework'[124] envisages that Member States preparation of future renewables plans should include consultation with neighbouring countries as a "key element", with a view to promoting market integration, improving cost-effectiveness and enhancing grid stability.[125]

Then, we should note that the details envisaged by the Commission in its 'policy framework' include a proposed '*iterative process*' concerning the drafting, development and assessment of 'National Renewable Energy Action Plans' (or NREAPs) (or whatever their equivalent might be called) under the 2030 framework. It is to be hoped that this may provide greater transparency for market actors and authorities in planning, assessing (etc.) projects: insofar as significant amounts of funding are expected to come from the private sector, transparency, clarity and predictability are going to be a crucial element if regulatory risks are to be mitigated and the cost of capital to finance such investment is to be minimised.

Is there a risk that this will serve to strengthen Commission oversight and control via State aid law *and* 'soft law' and 'governance' techniques, when it is not willing (or *able*?) to proceed via legislative harmonisation? To a point, this type of governance mechanism can be constructive and productive, in terms of improving our understanding of different ways of pursuing similar goals, learning lessons from the experiences of other Member States and being reminded to think about the potential impact of national policies beyond one country's borders. It is not clear whether, in its January 2014 policy framework, the Commission expected that the notification and assessment of national RES support schemes would form a particular part of this iterative process, but one could imagine that the information required from a Member State under this process would provide both a strong incentive for that government to examine its proposals closely from various angles, as well as offering extremely useful material from which the Commission could develop its own experience and, ultimately, guidance to Member States. *But* insofar as the strengthening of such Commission oversight and control amounts to securing legislative-style results while avoiding the safeguards and participation of that legislative process, this raises significant questions about the legitimacy and indeed legality of the Commission proceeding in this fashion, and links nicely to section IV 4, below.

---

123 See the contribution by C. König in this volume concerning offshore grids and some of the regulatory and legal issues which their development is already raising. (CK 3.1 and 3.2) p.

124 COM(2014) 15, fn. 98, above.

125 *Ibid.*, p. 13.

4. Article 194 TFEU and the new EEAG?

The preceding discussion has led us to the point where we need to consider possible links between the content and approach of the EEAG, on the one hand, and the meaning and implications of Article 194 TFEU (the new – since the Treaty of Lisbon – EU energy provision), on the other. Potential concerns *vis-à-vis* Article 194 TFEU arise for two main reasons.

First, some measure of democratic scrutiny and accountability via the ordinary legislative procedure is safeguarded by the wording of Article 194(2)'s first sentence, ensuring the involvement (and indeed requiring the final approval) of the European Parliament in the process of adopting EU-level energy legislation, including measures which "(a) ensure the functioning of the energy market; … and (c) promote … the development of … new and renewable forms of energy" (Article 194(1) TFEU). To pursue what we have suggested in the preceding suggestion appear to be legislative-style results through the expedient of State aid policy-making might be seen unjustifiably to avoid Parliamentary and, indeed, Member State scrutiny and prerogatives safeguarded by the TFEU itself. Here, a series of parallels could be drawn with the Court's sensitivity to such questions of protecting prerogatives under the old E(E)C Treaty: it has been keen to defend the powers of the European Parliament against attempts by the Council (and Commission) to utilise law-making procedures which sought to avoid a (more) significant role for the Parliament.[126] The Court expressly emphasised that:

The consultation [of the European Parliament] provided for … is the means which allows the Parliament to play an actual part in the legislative process …. [I]t reflects … the fundamental democratic principle that the peoples should take part in the exercise of power through the intermediary of a representative assembly.[127]

Indeed, a judgment[128] specifically concerning the energy sector concluded that an attempt to base Regulation 617/2010/EU[129] (concerning the notification to the

126 Originally in Case 138/79 *Roquette Frères* [1980] ECR 3333 (where the European Parliament's right to be consulted was protected), and more strongly in Case C-300/89 *Commission* v. *Council* ('*Titanium Dioxide*') [1991] ECR I-2867 (where the European Parliament's right to deeper involvement via the co-operation process was safeguarded). For discussion of these issues of protection of prerogatives and institutional balance, see, e.g.: *Lenaerts & Verhoeven*, Institutional Balance as a Guarantee for Democracy in EU Governance, in Joerges & Dehousse (eds.), Good Governance in Europe's Integrated Market (Oxford: OUP, 2002), ch. 2.

127 Case 138/79, n. 39, above, para. 33.

128 Case C-490/10 *European Parliament* v. *Council* (6 September 2012).

129 [2010] OJ L180/7.

Commission of investment projects in energy infrastructure within the European Union) upon a little-used Treaty provision (Article 337 TFEU),[130] which would have excluded the European Parliament from the law-making process altogether, was impermissible. The Court held that Article 194 "constitutes the legal basis intended to apply to all acts adopted by the European Union in the energy sector ... subject to ... the more specific provisions laid down by the TFEU on energy" (such as Articles 122 and 170 TFEU, concerning severe difficulties in the supply of energy products, and trans-European networks, respectively).[131] Since the gathering of such infrastructure-related information was energy-specific and a prerequisite to the adoption of future EU measures concerning the internal energy market, security of energy supply, energy efficiency and renewables, the measure fell under Article 194 TFEU.[132]

Similarly, the Court has defended the role of EC institutions and powers in the face of Member State attempts in Council to operate under the Common Foreign and Security Policy, thus excluding the Parliament from the process.[133] And the Court has also on occasion restrained the Commission from seeking to assert exclusive EC competence over all trade-related activities so as to exclude the Member States from any role in concluding the agreement by which the EC was to join the World Trade Organisation:[134] in so doing, it served to protect the Member States' competence, requiring that international agreement to be concluded by each of the Member States individually, as well as by the Commission on behalf of the EC.

These considerations have even been used by the Parliament and the Member States politically, so as to pressure the Commission into abandoning its original

130 Which allows the Commission, "within the limits and under the conditions laid down by the Council acting by a simple majority ..., collect any information and carry out any checks required for the performance of the tasks entrusted to it".

131 Case C-490/10, fn. 125, above, para. 67.

132 *Ibid.*, paras. 68–74, 79.

133 See, on the point of principle, Case C-170/96 *Commission* v. *Council* (*'Airport Transit Visas'*) [1998] ECR I-2763 and, for a practical example, Case C-70/94 *Werner* v. *Germany* [1995] ECR I-3189, where a sanctions measure which had as its effect the restriction of exports was held not to fall beyond the scope of the common commercial policy (an EC competence) simply because it pursued foreign policy and security objectives (a CFSP issue). See, now, Article 40 TEU: "[t]he implementation of the common foreign and security policy shall not affect the application of the procedures and the extent of the powers of the institutions laid down by the Treaties for the exercise of the Union competences referred to in Articles 3 to 6 of the TFEU".

134 Opinion 1/94 *Accession to the World Trade Organisation* [1994] ECR I-5267.

plan to pursue its internal energy market legislative programme in the early 1990s on the basis of Article 90(3) EEC (now, Article 106(3) TFEU.[135] Instead of using the EEC's legislative procedures which would have involved the Council and, to some extent at least, the European Parliament, Article 90(3) EEC would have allowed the Commission simply to adopt directives itself: while it would no doubt have intended extensive consultation and interaction with the other institutions in developing such legislation, the far-reaching and controversial nature of such liberalisation proposals ultimately required the use of the co-decision procedure under the old Article 189b EC, using Articles 57(2), 66 and 100a EC[136] as the legal basis for the first two internal energy market Directives.[137]

Second, and to emphasise the point about the protection of prerogatives even more strongly, we must consider the implications of the second sentence of Article 194(2) and the caveat which it contains. That caveat provides that:

> *Such measures shall not affect a Member State's right to determine the conditions for exploiting its energy resources, its choice between different energy sources and the general structure of its energy supply, without prejudice to Article 192(2)(c).*

For ease of reference, we shall refer to these three elements as Member State 'energy rights'. Whatever the phrase "shall not affect" is taken to mean,[138] it seems tolerably clear that this caveat was intended to offer the Member States some degree of protection against far-reaching EU-level measures which would have an impact upon those energy rights. Simply to sidestep such protection by relying upon the issue of guidelines under State aid law would seem questionable at best, especially when the result of the EEAG so clearly seems to operate as a genuinely significant restriction upon at least the first two of these energy rights, and quite possibly affects the third in no small way as well. In response to these criticisms, it might first be argued that a simple linguistic device could allow us (and the Commission!) to avoid all criticism of the EEAG based upon Article 194(2)'s caveat. This is because Article 194(2)'s second sentence refers to "such measures", which presumably must be taken to refer to measures adopted on the basis of Article 194(2)'s first sentence. Indeed, this was how the General Court[139] brushed off an

---

135 See n. 23, above, and the references cited therein.

136 Which concerned establishment (now Article 53 TFEU), services (now Article 62 TFEU) and the internal market (now Article 114 TFEU), respectively.

137 Directives 96/92/EC and 98/30/EC, fn. 23, above.

138 For extensive discussion and some tentative suggestions, see Johnston & van der Marel, '*Ad Lucem?*', n. 8, above.

139 In Case T-370/11 *Commission* v. *Poland* (7 March 2013).

attempt by Poland to argue that the Commission's Decision 2011/278/EU[140] – which determined EU-wide rules harmonising the free allocation of emissions allowances under the EU's emissions trading system (ETS) – had infringed all three of Poland's energy rights under Article 194(2)'s caveat.[141] The General Court simply noted that the EU's ETS Directive 2003/87/EC had been adopted on the basis of what was now Article 192(1) TFEU and was thus an environmental policy measure, not one adopted under Article 194(2)'s first paragraph.[142] Since Article 194 post-dates nearly all EU legislation and guidance on energy law in general, the broader implications of this argument are potentially far-reaching. Further, since the EEAG themselves are not adopted on the basis of Article 194 *at all*, it might be concluded that any attempt to criticise the EEAG for failing to respect the Member States' 'energy rights' as adumbrated in the second sentence of Article 194(2) is doomed to failure. It is respectfully submitted that this conclusion would be altogether too quick and insensitive to the reasons behind the inclusion of the caveat in the first place: clearly, the intention was in some way to protect the Member States from far-reaching intrusions into key aspects of national energy policy. Insofar as the EU judicature has consistently preferred arguments of substance over form,[143] allowing the Commission to sidestep this protection for Member States via such formalistic reasoning would be an unfortunate outcome.

Second, one might take the view that the serious uncertainty surrounding the meaning of the caveat to Article 194(2) TFEU would suggest, *normatively*, that it would be better to allow progress to be made in this area via the device of State aid guidelines and, ultimately, legislation (eventually in the form of a Block Exemption regulation, perhaps). If one were focused solely upon the ease of passing EU-level (legislative) measures in the energy field, then this argument could seem attractive, and it would rely at least in part upon the suggestions made earlier (section II 1,

---

140 [2011] OJ L130/1 (27 April 2011).

141 Poland's argument was that focusing upon natural gas to define emission benchmarks was unjustified when applied to countries (like itself) where coal was the dominant energy source used in electricity generation. The result, according to Poland, would be to disadvantage coal-fired generation and ultimately lead to increasing Poland's need to import natural gas, thereby disrupting its energy balance and requiring a redefinition of its overall energy policy: Case T-370/11 (n. 136, above), para. 10.

142 *Ibid.*, paras. 11–17.

143 See, e.g., the question of what amounts to a 'reviewable act' under Article 263 TFEU: despite taking the form of an internal instruction, where an act had definite legal effects by defining the powers of officials *vis-à-vis* third parties, it was reviewable (Case C-366/88 *France* v. *Commission* ('*Re EAGGF*') [1990] ECR I-3571).

above) that one must always be sensitive to the institutional and structural legal context within which such measures must be adopted and applied. Yet if one were concerned that State aid-driven policy- and law-making in this area runs the risk of failing to address important elements of energy and/or environmental policy, then relying upon this route would raise genuine concerns: arguably, the criticisms developed above concerning the substance and approach of the EEAG show that such fears are by no means misplaced. However much one might be frustrated by the delays, bargaining and (sometimes grubby) compromises which characterise EU-level law-making, the need to ensure that the EU's laws and policies – and especially in such a controversial field as renewable energy subsidies – are viewed as legitimate[144] is of crucial importance.

V. Conclusions

When considering the impact of EU law in general, and the rules and guidelines on State aid in particular, upon renewable energy law and policy, we must remember the legal structure, institutional powers/roles laid down by the Treaties, as well as the substantive and procedural law. This helps us to appreciate the contributions that may be made by the different institutions at different levels of practice, as well as the potential frictions between approaches (European and national, political and judicial, etc.).

Energy Subsidies raise State aid law concerns, of course, *but* pressures from other areas of EU law (e.g. free movement) may yet prove just as far-reaching: even though some of the pressure might have been relieved by the outcome in *Ålands Vindkraft* and *Essent Belgium*, the approach taken by the national courts when ruling upon the application of environmental justifications of national renewables support schemes will be crucial to their future scope and practical operation. Indeed, the involvement of courts (EU and national) can be a force for good in this area, by developing enforcement tools and reinforcing scrutiny of EU- and national-level law and policy-making. But developing renewables governance through court judgments can also have negative consequences: uncertainty may be engendered by specific rulings and their possible wider implications, and certain

144 In terms of the inputs into that law-making (consultation, public scrutiny, representative democratic participation and oversight) as well as the outputs thereof: for a brief outline of these legitimacy questions, see *Johnston*, "Euro-visions"? Some Thoughts on Prospects and Mechanisms for Future Constitutional Change in the European Union', in C. Barnard (ed.), The Fundamentals of EU Law Revisited: Assessing the Impact of the Constitutional Debate (OUP, 2007), ch. 8, at 255–258 and the references cited therein.

economic and policy analysts often criticise the courts for their overly 'legalistic' and technical approaches to particular issues so far as subsidies are concerned.

Finally, the new EEAG have to be seen as a real curate's egg: good in some parts, bad in others. They promise to enhance the Commission's role (in co-ordination with the RES 2030 proposals), constrain some Member States' approaches and have already raised criticism on competence and substantive grounds. Indeed, proceedings have now been initiated by the European Renewable Energy Federation before the EU's General Court to challenge the validity of the EEAG:[145] details of the grounds of challenge are not yet publicly available, but it is to be hoped that some of the issues canvassed in this contribution will be raised and analysed by the Court in due course.

145 Case T-694/14 *EREF* v. *Commission* (proceedings lodged, 22 September 2014).

Juliane Steffens
PhD Researcher at Enreg Institute of Energy and Regulatory Law, Berlin
steffens@enreg.eu

Articles 30 and 110 TFEU as Limitations to Member States' Renewable Energy Promotion

Content

I. Introduction

How are Member States bound in designing national schemes for the promotion of electricity from Renewable Energy Sources (RES)? State aid law in Articles 107 and 108 TFEU is the most prominent boundary. The fiscal provisions in Articles 30 and 110 TFEU have long been dwarfed by State aid law and the free movement of goods. With the *Essent Netwerk* case and selected decisions the Commission issued those provisions also moved into the focus of State aid control in the energy sector.

Article 107 TFEU as well as Article 30 and 110 TFEU are aimed at securing a level playing field for undertakings in the internal market; the latter more specifically target the free movement of goods.[1] State aid rules accomplish their aim by prohibiting aid measures to certain undertakings that distort or threaten to distort competition. Article 30 TFEU forbids customs duties and measures having equivalent effect. Article 110 TFEU demands indirect tax measures levied on products in the widest sense[2] to be fiscally neutral, which is often also coined competition neutrality.[3] However, Article 110 TFEU leaves national fiscal autonomy untouched as long as Member States levy products according to objective criteria irrespective of origin.[4]

In the following, the respective scope of Articles 107 and 110 will shortly be outlined to explain how those two notions are intertwined. After that, the Commission's case practice in the renewable energy sector shall be further examined before two landmark cases of State aid control in the energy sector are commented on.

---

1 Case 148/77 *Hansen/Hauptzollamt Flensburg* [1978] ECR 1788, para. 14: State aid provisions "also rest on the same basic idea as Article [110], namely the elimination of State interventions [...] which might have the effect of distorting the normal conditions of trade between Member States.", Case C-206/06 *Essent Netwerk Noord* [2008] ECR I-5497, para. 60.

2 That includes charges on "necessary activit[ies] in connection with the product" such as transport, Case C-206/06 *Essent Netwerk Noord* [2008] ECR I-5497, para. 44.

3 *Barents*, The Prohibition of Fiscal Discrimination in Article 95 of the EEC Treaty, CMLRev 1980, 437, 443; *Englisch*, Wettbewerbsgleichheit im grenzüberschreitenden Handel. Mit Schlussfolgerungen für indirekte Steuern, (Mohr Siebeck, 2008).

4 *Barnard*, The Substantive Law of the European Union. The Four Freedoms, (OUP, 4th ed. 2013), p. 53 f.; *Easson*, Fiscal discrimination: New Perspectives on Article 95 of the EEC Treaty, CMLRev 1981, 521, 540 f.

II. The interplay between Articles 107 and 110 TFEU

Before we can further examine the interplay of Article 107 TFEU and the prohibition of internal discriminating tax measures according to Article 110 TFEU, their respective scopes of application shall be outlined as far as it is necessary for the purpose of this paper.

1. Scope of Article 110 TFEU

Article 110(1) TFEU forbids Member States to impose, directly or indirectly, on the products of other Member States any internal taxation of any kind in excess of that imposed directly or indirectly on similar domestic products. First, as the wording "internal" suggest, Article 110 TFEU catches national measures applying to domestic and foreign products alike.[5] This distinguishes Article 110's scope from that of Article 30 TFEU.[6] Customs duties and charges having equivalent effect are levied on imported or exported products only, they either legally or factually discriminate and are charged because products cross a border ("cross border causality").[7] Only in exceptional cases measures falling prima facie under Article 110 TFEU, because they levy domestic and foreign products alike, are in fact caught by Article 30 TFEU: When Member States fully offset the duties national producers have to pay foreign products alone are left to pay the charge which, thus, has the effect of a customs duty.[8]

The phrase "Any internal taxation of any kind" tells us that Member States' measures falling under Article 110 TFEU are not limited to tax provisions in the strict sense, i.e. provisions that generate income for the State. In fact, Article 110

5 See e.g. Cases C-393/04 and 41/05 *Air Liquide Industries Belgium* [2006] ECR I-5293, para. 55; case C-206/06 *Essent Netwerk Noord* ECR 2008, I-5497, para. 41; *Barents,* The Prohibition of Fiscal Discrimination in Article 95 of the EEC Treaty, CMLRev 1980, p. 437, 438.

6 Case 78/76 *Steinike & Weinlig* [1977] ECR 595, para. 28; case C-77/72 *Capolongo/ Azienda Agricola Maya* [1973] ECR 611, para. 18; case C-206/06 *Essent Netwerk Noord* [2008] ECR I-5497, para. 41; cases C-393/04 and 41/05 *Air Liquide Industries Belgium* [2006] ECR I-5293, paras. 51 and 55 f.

7 Case C-234/99 *Nygård* [2002] ECR I-3657, para. 19; case C-355/00 *Freskot* [2003] ECR I-5263, para. 42. See further *Barents,* The Prohibition of Fiscal Discrimination in Article 95 of the EEC Treaty, CMLRev 1980, p. 437, 438.

8 Case 78/76 *Steinike & Weinlig* [1977] ECR 595, para. 28; case 78/90 *Compagnie commerciale de l'Ouest* [1992] ECR I-1847, para. 27; case C-206/06 *Essent Netwerk Noord* [2008] ECR I-5497, para. 42.

TFEU also covers so called parafiscal levies[9] or other special charges, that are earmarked for a special purpose and do not form part of the State's general budget. In its first section Article 110 TFEU forbids the discrimination of imported products with regard to similar domestic products – the tax on the imported product must not be higher; section 2 forbids the discrimination of imported products being in competition with other domestic goods.[10] A directly discriminating tax on similar products is prohibited per se[11] whereas differentiating tax measures might be allowed under section 1 if the Member State invokes an objective unrelated to origin that is recognized by EU law and the measure is proportionate.[12] The CJEU interprets section 2 to only forbid the discriminating element of a tax measure. Although the CJEU demanded that Member States extend a tax advantage for domestic products to imported products[13] it is within the Member States' discretion how to remove a particular discrimination.[14] They may either level up or level down the benefit conferred to domestic products.[15] With those different legal consequences – per se prohibition of different taxation and abolition of the discriminating element – a so called global approach[16] where no distinction need

9 This terminology refers to the German "Sonderabgaben" or "parafiskalische Abgaben" as well as the French "taxes parafiscales", for more charges in different Member States see *Jaeger,* Beihilfen durch Steuern und parafiskalische Abgaben, NWV Neuer Wiss. Verl., 2006, p. 275 ff.; *Jaeger,* in: Frank Montag/Franz Jürgen Säcker (ed.), Münchener Kommentar zum europäischen und deutschen Wettbewerbsrecht. Band 3: Beihilfen- und Vergaberecht, (C.H. Beck, 2011), E. Steuerliche Maßnahmen, para. 15.

10 For the question whether section 1 is applicable in cases of no corresponding domestic production *Barbara Balke,* Steuerliche Gestaltungsfreiheit der Mitgliedstaaten und freier Warenverkehr im europäischen Binnenmarkt, Nomos, 1998, p. 130 ff.

11 Case 148/77 *Hansen/Hauptzollamt Flensburg* [1978] ECR 1788, para. 19; *René Barents,* The Prohibition of Fiscal Discrimination in Article 95 of the EEC Treaty, CMLRev 1980, p. 437, 440 ff.

12 See further *Barnard,* The Substantive Law of the European Union. The Four Freedoms (OUP, 4th ed. 2013), p. 66; *Easson,* Fiscal discrimination: New Perspectives on Article 95 of the EEC Treaty, CMLRev 1981, p. 521, 540 ff.

13 Case 148/77 *Hansen/Hauptzollamt Flensburg* [1978] ECR 1788, para. 17: "However, according to the requirements of Article 95, such preferential systems must be extended without discrimination to spirits coming from other Member States." In this case, however, the CJEU did not differentiate between sections 1 and 2.

14 *Easson,* Fiscal discrimination: New Perspectives on Article 95 of the EEC Treaty, CMLRev 1981, p. 521, 541 differing.

15 *Barnard,* The Substantive Law of the European Union. The Four Freedoms, (OUP, 4th ed. 2013), p. 65.

16 *Ibid.*

be made between the two sections cannot be followed.[17] In the energy sector, tax systems and systems of special charges are equally prevalent. The financial impact on consumers is greater in systems of special charges. Thus, taxation systems and exemptions thereof will not be treated in this article.[18]

2. Scope of Article 107 TFEU

Article 107(1) TFEU prohibits Member States from granting financial aid to undertakings to prevent competition between Member States from being distorted. Four cumulative criteria have to be fulfilled, namely (1) an economic advantage has to be conferred (2) by the State or through State resources to (3) selective undertakings and (4) distort or threaten to distort competition. National measures prone to involve State aid must be notified with the Commission before they may enter into force. Article 108(1) and (3) TFEU grant the Commission a right of first access – of ex ante scrutiny whether Member States' measures are in conflict with the substantive law of Article 107 TFEU. As long as Member States provisions are not cleared by the Commission, governments, institutions, and courts have to withhold implementation (standstill obligation, Article 108(3) TFEU).[19]

State involvement has been a particularly troublesome element in the substantive programme of Article 107 TFEU – first and foremost because it directly reflects on the allocation of competences between the Commission and the Member States; secondly, because it provides the breeding grounds for a link between

---

17 *Balke*, Steuerliche Gestaltungsfreiheit der Mitgliedstaaten und freier Warenverkehr im europäischen Binnenmarkt, Nomos, 1998, p. 139 f.

18 For a more detailed account on those issues see *Schön*, State Aid in the Area of Taxation, in: Leigh Hancher/Tom Ottervanger/Pieter J. Slot (eds.): EU State Aids, (Sweet & Maxwell, 4th ed. 2012), ch. 10 (pp. 321 ff.); *Jaeger*, in: Frank Montag/Franz Jürgen Säcker (ed.), Münchener Kommentar zum europäischen und deutschen Wettbewerbsrecht. Band 3: Beihilfen- und Vergaberecht, (C.H. Beck, 2011), E. Steuerliche Maßnahmen; *Flett/Walkerova*, An Ecotax under the State Aid Spotlight: The UK Aggregates Levy, in: Alastair Sutton (ed.): EC State aid law. Le Droit des Aides d'Etat dans la CE. Liber Amicorum Francisco Santaolalla Gadea, (Kluwer Law Internat, 2008), pp. 223 ff. Especially in relation to exemptions from energy related special charges and environmental taxes the criterion of selectivity has been subject to discussion: See e.g. *Ahlin* Material Selectivity, a Less Fuzzy Concept?, EStAL 2012, p. 847; *Bartosch*, Is There a Need for a Rule of Reason in European State Aid Law? Or How to Arrive at a Coherent Concept of Material Selectivity?, CMLRev 2010, p. 729; *Lopéz*, General Thoughts in Selectivity and Consequences of a Broad Concept of State Aid in tax Matters, EStAL 2010, p. 807; *Traversa*, Tax Amnesties of EU Member States and Their Compatibility with EU Law, (Intertax 2010), p. 239.

19 See also the contribution by Johnston in this volume (*Johnston*, section II 2 a).

State aid control and fiscal measures. It is this nexus between involvement of State resources and the imposition of special levies we shall now turn to.[20]

3. Where they meet: Article 107 (1) TFEU «by a Member State or through State Resources»

a) *The twofold State test of Article 107 (1) TFEU*

The standard test of whether a measure is "granted by a Member State or through State resources" comprises two elements: First, monies have to be State resources; second, the transfer decision of those monies must flow from the State.[21] Thus, the text of the Treaty has been construed to mean "by a Member State AND through State resources".[22] As a consequence, one could speak of a "State-test" as an overall concept. In those languages providing an adjective to "State" either this or its nominalisation should adequately coin the CJEU's overall concept of Article 107(1)'s criteria "by the State or through State resources".[23]

If the State does not directly act through its authorities, but e.g. through public undertakings, the concrete exercise of influence on the transfer decision must be carved out. The criteria laid down in *Stardust*[24] indicate the degree of State control and whether the undertaking acted autonomously. It is, however, the same criterion,

---

20 *Jaeger,* in: Frank Montag/Franz Jürgen Säcker (ed.), Münchener Kommentar zum europäischen und deutschen Wettbewerbsrecht. Band 3: Beihilfen- und Vergaberecht, (C.H. Beck, 2011), E. Steuerliche Maßnahmen, para. 16; *Hancher/Salerno,* State aid in the energy sector, in: Szyszczak (ed.): Research Handbook on European State Aid Law, Edward Elgar, 2011, p. 246 ff., para. 5.256: "The case law in this area is notoriously opaque".

21 Case C-482/99 *France/Commission (Stardust Marine)* [2002] ECR I-4397, para. 24; case C-677/11 *Doux Élevages and Coopérative agricole UKL-AREE* EuZW 2011, 582, para. 27; case C-262/12 *Vent De Colère!* EuZW 2014, 115, para. 16; see also *Rusche/Micheau/Piffaut/van de Casteele,* State Aid, in: Jonathan Faull/Ali Nikpay (eds.): The EU law of competition, (OUP, 3rd ed. 2014), p. 1923 ff., para. 17.22; *Heidenhain*, European State aid law, (Beck, 2010), § 4 para. 29; *Schmid-Kühnhöfer,* Die Staatlichkeit von Beihilfen. Mittel- und Transferzurechnung nach Art. 87 Abs. 1 EG-Vertrag, (P. Lang, 2004), p. 101 ff.

22 Case C-262/12 *Vent De Colère!* EuZW 2014, 115, para. 16; *Rusche/Micheau/Piffaut/van de Casteele,* State Aid, in: Faull/Nikpay (eds.): The EU law of competition, (OUP, 3rd ed. 2014), p. 1923 ff., at para. 17.20; *Heidenhain*, European State aid law, (Beck, 2010), § 4 at para. 30.

23 German: staatlich, Staatlichkeit; Bokmål: statlig.

24 Case C-482/99 *France/Commission (Stardust Marine)* [2002] ECR I-4397.

namely that of public control, which attributes private monies to the State.[25] Private money can amount to State resources as long as it comes under public control and is available to public authorities or publicly controlled undertakings.[26] The amounts do not formally have to become part of the national budget or be held by the Treasury.[27] Thus, in cases where private bodies confer private money (e.g. the grid operators pay premiums or feed-in tariffs to plant operators and invoice an extra charge from consumers) the State has to exert abstract control over the private bodies as well as the concrete act of transfer (as it was required in *Stardust Marine*). However, one caveat still remains: The Stardust case was concerned with an individual aid measure, whereas promotion systems for renewable energies are aid schemes. Not only Article 1 of the Procedural Regulation (Reg. No 659/1999)[28] differentiates between individual aids (Article 1(e))[29] and aid schemes (Article 1(d)).[30] Consequently, the obligation to prove State control – in addition to abstract corporate law control – differs, too. The Commission may resort to controlling the general elements of an aid scheme; it does not have to assess every

25 *Jaeger*, Beihilfen durch Steuern und parafiskalische Abgaben, (NWV Neuer Wiss. Verl., 2006), p. 268.

26 Case 173/73 *Italy/Commission* [1974] ECR 709, para. 16; Case 78/76 *Steinike & Weinlig* [1977] ECR 595, para. 21; *Rusche/Micheau/Piffaut/van de Casteele*, State Aid, in: Jonathan Faull/Ali Nikpay (eds.): The EU law of competition, (OUP, 3rd ed. 2014), p. 1923 ff., paras. 17.23–26; in opposition to that *Soltész*, in: Montag/Säcker (ed.), Münchener Kommentar zum europäischen und deutschen Wettbewerbsrecht. Band 3: Beihilfen- und Vergaberecht, (C.H. Beck, 2011), Article 107, para. 240.

27 Case 290/83 *Commission/France (CNCA)* [1985] ECR 439, para. 14: „As is clear from the actual wording of Article [110](1), aid need not necessarily be financed from State resources to be classified as State aid."

28 Of 22 March 1999, OJ L 83/1, 27.3.1999, last amended by Council Regulation (EU) No 734/2013 of 22 July 2013 OJ L 204/15, 31.7.2013.

29 "'individual aid' shall mean aid that is not awarded on the basis of an aid scheme and notifiable awards of aid on the basis of an aid scheme."

30 "'aid scheme' shall mean any act on the basis of which, without further implementing measures being required, individual aid awards may be made to undertakings defined within the act in a general and abstract manner and any act on the basis of which aid which is not linked to a specific project may be awarded to one or several undertakings for an indefinite period of time and/or for an indefinite amount."

single payment in detail.[31] The degree of control, thus, depends on the concrete design of the laws enacting a financing system for renewable energies.[32]

b) *State resources as a normative concept*

Case-law has shown time and again that the notion of "State resources" is a normative concept. We can see in *Air France v. Commission* that it was sufficient for the State to control a mere *credit balance* rather than individualised private amounts of money.[33] Similarly, unclaimed winnings in the *Ladbroke racing* case were considered to be State resources irrespective of being actually transferred to the Treasury.[34] Also, the foregoing of merely *potential* auction proceeds in the Dutch NOx case shows that the control criterion entails a normative element.[35] This element has its roots in the effects based approach.[36] The decisive factor for the normative attribution to the State is not, as many authors assert,[37] whether the Treasury has suffered any losses,[38] but whether monies were under public

---

31 Case 248/84 *Germany/Commission* [1987] ECR 4013, para. 18 concerning a regional aid programme; C-75/97, ECR 1999 I-03671, para. 48 – Belgium/Commission concerning a degressive system of social security contributions ("Maribel"); case C-15/98 *Italy and Sardegna Lines/Commission* [2000] ECR I-08855, para. 51 concerning a supporting fund for the Sardinian shipping sector.

32 See *Steffens*, in: Berliner Kommentar zum Energierecht, Vol. 2, 2nd ed. 2013, Einleitung EEG.

33 Case T-358/94 *Air France/Kommission* [1996] ECR II-2112, para. 67.

34 Case C-83/98 P *France/Ladbroke Racing and Commission* [2000] ECR I-3271, paras. 49 f.

35 Case C-279/08 P *Commission/Netherlands (NOx emission trading)* [2011] ECR I-7471, para. 107.

36 Case C-677/11 *Doux Élevages and Coopérative agricole UKL-AREE*, EuZW 2011, 582, paras. 36–40; case C-345/02 *Pearle* [2004] ECR I-7139, para. 37.

37 *Soltész*, in: Frank Montag/Franz Jürgen Säcker (ed.), Münchener Kommentar zum europäischen und deutschen Wettbewerbsrecht. Band 3: Beihilfen- und Vergaberecht, (C.H. Beck, 2011), Article 107, para. 240 who states that the twofold test was comprised of an imputable transfer and a loss to the budget. This is misleading as *Soltész* takes the causality test which is an inherent element of the control criterion and inaccurately makes it the starting point of the twofold State test. Insecure *Heidenhain*, European State aid law, (C.H. Beck, 2010), § 4 para. 29.

38 This, in fact, contradicts settled case law: case 290/83 *Commission/France (CNCA)* [1985] ECR 439, para. 14: "As is clear from the actual wording of Article [110](1), aid need not necessarily be financed from State resources to be classified as State aid." Case C-279/08 P *Commission/Netherlands (NOx emission trading)* [2011] ECR I-7471, para. 104. See also *Bartosch*, EU-Beihilfenrecht. Kommentar; Art. 86–89 EGV, De-minimis-Verordnung,

control.[39] Foregoing State revenue may serve as an indicator for public control but is not necessary to establish it. This coherently explains the CJEU's Statement that "it is not necessary to establish in every case that there has been a transfer of State resources".[40] Instead Article 107(1) TFEU "*covers all the financial means by which the public sector may actually support undertakings, irrespective of whether or not those means are permanent assets of the public sector.*"[41] Lastly, it is misleading to regard imputability and control as two distinct tests.[42] The exertion of control is the very reason for monies to be imputable to the State; only when the State can use resources as its own means a payment to selected undertakings may fall under State aid rules.[43]

The above mentioned examples show one important thing: It is the amplitude of fiscal power the State broadens by controlling private monies which it then may use to influence market processes.[44] State control is a powerful tool and detector for potential interferences with competition. Consequently, private undertakings collecting funds on their own initiative and for their own purpose are not

---

Allgemeine Gruppenfreistellungsverordnung sowie Verfahrensverordnung, (C.H. Beck, 2009), Art. 87 Abs. 1 para. 122 who rightly states that the loss to the budget is merely incidental to the control exerted by the State – not the other way round; *Hancher*, The General Framework, in: Hancher/Ottervanger/Slot (eds.): EU State Aids, (Sweet & Maxwell, 4th ed. 2012), para. 3–022. In contrast to that see *Soltész*, in: *Montag/Säcker* (ed.), Münchener Kommentar zum europäischen und deutschen Wettbewerbsrecht. Band 3: Beihilfen- und Vergaberecht, (C.H. Beck, 2011), Art. 107, para. 240; *Soltész*, Wann ist eine Beihilfe "staatlich"? – Das Kriterium der "Zurechenbarkeit" nach Stardust, ZWeR 2010, 198, 199 f.; *Soltész*, Die Entwicklung des europäischen Beihilferechts im Jahr 2013, EuZW 2014, 89, 90 f.

39 See for that *Säcker/Schmitz (married Steffens)*, Die Staatlichkeit der Mittel im Beihilfenrecht, NZKart 2014, p. 202; Early *Kühling*, Von den Vergütungspflichten des Energieeinspeisungsgesetzes bis zur Deckungsvorsorge des Atomgesetzes: Die deutsche Energierechtsordnung im Koordinatensystem des Europäischen Beihilfenrechts, RdE 2001, 93, 96 f.

40 Case C-677/11 *Doux Élevages and Coopérative agricole UKL-AREE* EuZW 2011, 582, para. 34.

41 Case T-358/94 *Air France/Commission* [1996] II-2112, para. 67.

42 *Flavia Tomat*, State Resources and Imputability to the State: A Clarification on the Scope of the Pearle Judgment?, EStAL 2014, p. 540, 544 ff.

43 This *Flavia Tomat*, State Resources and Imputability to the State: A Clarification on the Scope of the Pearle Judgment?, EStAL 2014, p. 540, 545, esp. fn. 33 also suspects since she correctly observes that indicators to establish imputability and control substantially overlap.

44 See BerlKommEnR/*Steffens*, Vol. II., 3rd ed. 2015, Einleitung EEG, paras. 110 ff.

measured against Article 107(1)[45] but rather find their limits in Articles 101 and 102 TFEU. They underlie State aid rules, however, when they function as mere "instruments" of the State – whether they are private or public undertakings.[46] It is submitted that renewable promotion schemes are without exception initiated by the State, meticulously planned, and in most cases backed up by administrative sanctions.

c) *Differentiated test for parafiscal levies financing aid*

Why is the State resources test so hard in cases of special charges and parafiscal levies? First, it is because of the numerous fashions in which Member States can draw up collection systems – State control has to be established on a case to case basis. However, the Court has held in *France v. Commission*[47] as well as in *Iannelli*[48] and *Steinike*[49] that monies stemming from a levy generally fall within the scope of Article 107(1) TFEU.[50] It has reinforced this notion in later judgments.[51] For a tax measure or a charge to be State aid the four criteria of State aid cumulatively

45 Case C-345/02 *Pearle* [2004] ECR I-7139, para. 37.

46 Case C-677/11 *Doux Élevages and Coopérative agricole UKL-AREE* EuZW 2011, 582, para. 40: "instruments"; case C-345/02 *Pearle* [2004] ECR I-7139, para. 37: "vehicle"; *Soltész,* in: Montag/Säcker (ed.), Münchener Kommentar zum europäischen und deutschen Wettbewerbsrecht. Band 3: Beihilfen- und Vergaberecht, C.H. Beck, 2011, Art. 107, para. 244: "Erfüllungsgehilfe" (agent).

47 Case 47/69 *France/Commission* [1970] ECR 487, paras. 11 ff.

48 Case C-74/76 *Iannelli & Volpi/Meroni* [1977] ECR 557, para. 14.

49 Case 78/76 *Steinike & Weinlig* [1977] ECR 595, para. 22: "[a] measure adopted by the public authority and favouring certain undertakings or products does not lose the character of a gratuitous advantage by the fact that it is wholly or partially financed by contributions imposed by the public authority and levied on the undertakings concerned." In later decisions the CJEU has more clearly differentiated between the economic advantage conferred to undertakings and the involvement of State resources. Today, the question whether the disbursement of a levy is an advantage is assessed according to the private investor test. Economically sound consideration for a service is no advantage. See *Jaeger*, in: Frank Montag/Franz Jürgen Säcker (ed.), Münchener Kommentar zum europäischen und deutschen Wettbewerbsrecht. Band 3: Beihilfen- und Vergaberecht, C.H. Beck, 2011, E. Steuerliche Maßnahmen, para. 83.

50 Case C- 17/91 *Lornoy* [1992] ECR I-6523, para. 32; case C-72/92 *Scharbatke/Germany* [1993] ECR I-5509, paras. 18 and 20; case C-234/99 *Nygård* [2002] ECR I-3657, para. 53; case C-206/06 *Essent Netwerk Noord* [2008] ECR I-5497, para. 59.

51 Case 289/85 *France/Commission (DEFI)* [1987] ECR 4393, para. 23; case C-234/99 *Nygård* [2002] ECR I-3657, para. 53; case C-72/92 *Scharbatke/Germany* [1993] ECR I-5509, paras. 18 and 20.

have to be met. Articles 30 or 110 TFEU and Article 107 TFEU are both applicable: Article 107(2) and (3) TFEU govern the revenues' usage whereas discriminatory collection modalities are prevented by Articles 30 and 110 TFEU.[52] While the State origin of tax measures is hardly questionable, the State character of special levies has proven to be one of the most arduous questions to answer in State aid control. It was the Commission that explicitly developed a **three criteria test** for parafiscal levies to become State resources: "[T]*he fund or account was created or designated by the State, that it is funded by contributions imposed by the State and that it is used to favour certain enterprises.*"[53]

Though the Commission invoked *Italy v. Commission* and *Steinike* – in an allegedly "constant practice of the Court"[54] – it was the Commission itself giving the State test its particular form. The Court lays down those three criteria rather vaguely. In *Commission/Italy*[55] it held:

> "*As the funds in question are financed through compulsory contributions imposed by State legislation and as, as this case shows, they are managed and apportioned in accordance with the provisions of that legislation, they must be regarded as State resources within the meaning of Article 92, even if they are administered by institutions distinct from the public authorities*".[56]

In *Steinike*[57] it held that sector specific charges collected by private undertakings can also amount to State resources simply because of their compulsory origin.[58] Supporting the effects based approach it purported that "*the status of the institutions entrusted with the distribution and administration of the aid*"[59] should be unimportant. Firstly, the funds have to be financed by the levy – that reproduces the case law concentrating on the hypothecation of proceeds and the appropriation

52 Case C-206/06 *Essent Netwerk Noord* [2008] ECR I-5497, para. 59.

53 Commission, decision dated 13.12.2001, NN 6/A/2001, para. 23 – Irish electricity out of peat.

54 Commission, decision dated 13.12.2001, NN 6/A/2001, para. 23 – Irish electricity out of peat.

55 Case 173/73 *Italy/Commission* [1974] ECR, 709.

56 Case 173/73 *Italy/Commission* [1974] ECR 709, para. 16.

57 Case 78/76 *Steinike & Weinlig* [1977] ECR 595.

58 Case 78/76 *Steinike & Weinlig* [1977] ECR 595, para. 22: "A measure adopted by the public authority and favouring certain undertakings or products does not lose the character of a gratuitous advantage by the fact that it is wholly or partially financed by contributions imposed by the public authority and levied on the undertakings concerned." That was reinforced later in Case C-206/06 *Essent Netwerk Noord* [2008] ECR I-5497, para. 66.

59 Case 78/76 *Steinike & Weinlig* [1977] ECR 595, para. 21.

of aid.[60] And, secondly, they have to be used in accordance with the legislative framework. The third element, namely that the State has to set up or designate a body and entrust it with the administration of the benefits, can only be distilled with some effort from the Court's obiter dictum. If the interplay between State aid rules and parafiscal financing mechanisms are rather poorly asserted by the Court, the historic development of parafiscal levies in State aid control has to be taken into account. Commission and Court adapted rather abruptly to the new dangers parafiscal levies posed to free trade late 1960's: The Commission, being alarmed by the increasing number of parafiscal charges financing aid, simply plead for their inclusion into State aid control.[61] Accordingly, in its early decisions it claims that parafiscal levies make State resources.[62] The Court followed suit in his early judgments.[63]

Today, the Commission repeatedly applies its three criteria test when assessing special charges in the energy sector. Until *PreussenElektra* the State mainly entrusted public corporations and authorities so that establishing public control always had a convincing starting point. With different designs of promotion schemes for renewable energies it has become more apparent that a grey area remains between State aid free private law obligations and State aid financed from parafiscal levies.

4. Procedural effects of parafiscal aid systems: concentration

This line between an aid-free transfer of private resources and public charges (either in the sense of Article 30 or 110 TFEU) is crucial because of the procedural

60 Case 74/76 *Iannelli & Volpi/Meroni* [1977] ECR 557, para. 14; case C-174/02 *Streekgewest* [2005] ECR I-85, para. 26; cases C-266/04 to C-270/04, C-276/04 and C-321/04 to C-325/04 *Distribution Casino France* [2005] ECR I-9481, para. 40; cases C-34/01 to C-38/01 *Enirisorse* [2003] ECR I-14243, para. 44.

61 Commission, Third General Report on the Activities of the Communities, 1969, p. 72: "In view of the growing number of aids financed from para-fiscal charges and of their effect on the establishment and functioning of the common market, the Commission proposes to check these aids systematically for compatibility with the EEC Treaty, particularly Articles 12, 95 and 92."

62 Commission, decision dated 18.7.1969, 69/266/EEC, OJ L 1969, 220/1, p. 2 – reorganisation in the textile industry; Commission, decision dated 6.12.1972, 72/436/EEC, OJ L 1972, 297/32, p. 33 – National forestry fund; in Commission, decision dated 17.12.1973, 74/8/EEC, OJ L 1974, 14/23 – Technical Centres, the quality of aid is not even explicitly Stated, but assumed, *Jaeger*, Beihilfen durch Steuern und parafiskalische Abgaben, (NWV Neuer Wiss. Verl., 2006), p. 284 f. with similar reasoning.

63 Case 173/73 *Italy/Commission* [1974] ECR 709.

control mechanisms those two systems entail: As the *PreussenElektra* case illustrated private obligations are subject to the procedural ex post review that hinges on Article 34 TFEU. In principle, Articles 30 and 110 TFEU are also subject to the Court's ex post review. The procedure to be followed in State aid control, however, is more onerous to Member States: they have to notify any measure to the Commission in advance according to Art. 108(3) TFEU (*ex ante* review) and must not implement any measure without the Commission's permission (standstill obligation). State aid procedure is at the sole competence of the Commission and the complex assessment procedure must not be undermined by infringement procedures.[64]

Substantive aid assessment according to Article 107(3) TFEU is at the Commission's discretion.[65] Where the revenue of a levy is hypothecated to an aid measure, i.e. mandatorily and exclusively used for conferring benefits to selected undertakings,[66] the Commission has to extend its assessment to Articles 30 and 110 TFEU.[67] The level of charges and the advantages conferred to selected undertakings have to correspond for the charge not to be severable from the aid purpose.[68] Once the financing mechanism is indispensable for the purpose of the aid measure, all relevant legal aspects are examined during the State aid procedure. But the Commission must not use its discretion to contravene other Treaty provisions.[69] Articles 30 and 110 TFEU form an objective limit to the Commission's discretion and forbid it to approve measures that may be in line with State aid objectives but perpetuate a discriminating financing scheme. Thus, in *France v. Commission* the CJEU has authorised the Commission to consider "all the legal and factual circumstances surrounding" an aid measure.[70]

Whether money is deployed in accordance with Union objectives is still subject to Article 107 (2) and (3) TFEU. Apart from that, the collection modalities of a surcharge underlie Articles 30 and 110 TFEU.[71] If a collection modality impinges

64 Not even through the Commission itself who is barred from initiating an infringement procedure according to Article 258 TFEU, see case 290/83 *Commission/France (CNCA)* [1985] ECR 439, para. 18 f.

65 Case 78/76 *Steinike & Weinlig* [1977] ECR 595, para. 8.

66 Cases C-261/01 and C-262/01 *van Calster und Cleeren* [2003] ECR I-12249, paras. 55 and 68.

67 Case C-206/06 *Essent Netwerk Noord* [2008] ECR I-5497, para. 59; case C-72/92 *Scharbatke/Germany* [1993] ECR I-5509, para. 18.

68 Case C-174/02 *Streekgewest* [2005] ECR I-85, para. 32.

69 Case C-234/99 *Nygård* [2002] ECR I-3657, para. 54.

70 Case 47/69 *France/Commission* [1970] ECR 487, para. 7.

71 Case C-206/06 *Essent Netwerk Noord* [2008] ECR I-5497, para. 59; case 73/79 *Italy/Commission* [1980] ECR 1534, para. 9.

Articles 30 or 110 TFEU, the Commission has to order a Member State to alter it.[72] Only then the Commission may issue a positive decision in its State aid assessment. For the Member States the standstill obligation in Article 108(3) TFEU extends to the collection of charges.[73]

However, State aid control does not prejudice judicial review following from the direct effect of Articles 30, 34 and 110 TFEU as long as elements can be assessed separately from an aid measure.[74] The Court often does not rule on whether Article 30 or 110 is applicable because this depends on factual circumstances that national courts are in a better position to assess.[75] Depending on whom those revenues benefit and to what extent, national courts are bound to decide whether Article 30 or 110 TFEU is applicable.[76] Thus, the Court regularly refers to them the application of Articles 30 and 110.[77] In the following I will turn to cases of renewable energy support systems in which the Commission considered Articles 30 and 110 TFEU.

III. The evolution of parafiscal levies in the energy sector: A Commission case history

1. Irish Peat (December 2001)

Shortly after the *PreussenElektra* decision was handed down the Commission issued several decisions on aid measures in the energy sector that were financed by special charges. Those decisions illustrate the fine line that the Commission was struggling to find between a series of judgments that was initiated by the Court long before *PreussenElektra* – namely that of *Italy v. Commission*[78], *Iannelli & Volpi*[79] and *Steinike & Weinlig*[80] – and the new ruling on minimum prices of the German Renewables Law. Just half a year after *PreussenElektra* the Commission

72 Case 47/69 *France/Commission* [1970] ECR 487, para. 9.

73 *Thomas Jaeger*, Beihilfen durch Steuern und parafiskalische Abgaben, NWV Neuer Wiss. Verl., 2006, p. 269 f. and p. 366 ff.; *Meyer*, Die Bewertung parafiskalischer Abgaben aus der Sicht des europäischen Beihilferechts, p. 227 ff.

74 Case 74/76 *Iannelli & Volpi/Meroni* [1977] ECR 557, para. 14.

75 Cases C-149/91 and C-150/91 *Sanders Adour* [1992] ECR I-3899, para. 18; case 78/90 *Compagnie commerciale de l'Ouest* [1992] ECR I-1847, para. 28.

76 Case C-77/72 *Capolongo/Azienda Agricola Maya* [1973] ECR 611, para. 12.

77 See only case C-206/06 *Essent Netwerk Noord* [2008] ECR I-5497, paras. 51 ff.

78 Case 173/73 *Italy/Commission* [1974] ECR 709.

79 Case 74/76 *Iannelli & Volpi/Meroni* [1977] ECR 557.

80 Case 78/76 *Steinike & Weinlig* [1977] ECR 595.

was concerned with the Irish system for promoting electricity out of peat that imposed a public service obligation on one supplier (the former incumbent Electricity Supply Board (EBS), still State owned at that time).[81] The extra costs of the obligation were computed by the Irish regulator[82] on a yearly basis; the transmission system operator was to collect a levy from all network subscribers with regard to their network capacity that should cover the extra costs.

Under the control of the regulator the TSO channeled the revenue it had collected into a separate account and from there to EBS. Any excess amount was offset against the levy in the forthcoming year – not as in the subsequent case *Essent Netwerk* – paid over to the government.

The Commission was openly insecure whether to assess this mechanism as including State resources. On the one hand it referred to *Italy v. Commission* and *Steinike* to reach the conclusion that State resources could be involved. On the other hand, the Commission surrendered to the conundrum the CJEU had evoked with *PreussenElektra* using the following words:

> *"In its ruling of 13 March 2001 in Case C-379/98 PreussenElektra AG, the Court established that a national law of a Member State, which requires private electricity supply undertakings to purchase electricity produced in their area of supply from renewable energy sources at minimum prices higher than the real economic value of that type of electricity, does not involve any direct or indirect transfer of State resources to undertakings which produce that type of electricity. Therefore, the Commission considers that it cannot be determined whether the notified scheme constitutes State aid in the meaning of Article 87(1) of the EC Treaty. Therefore, the Commission does not decide if the compensations are State aid in the meaning of Article 87(1) of the EC Treaty. Such a decision is not necessary as, in any case, as it will be demonstrated below, such a potential aid would be compatible with the EC Treaty."*[83]

Understandable as this insecurity is – and it once more shows how *PreussenElektra* did in fact mark a bifurcation in what otherwise would have been a continuous path of cases – the CJEU did not overrule *Commission v. Italy*, *Iannelli* and *Steinikein PreussenElektra*.[84] Instead of turning over *Steinike* it reinforced the phrase

81 Commission, decision dated 13.12.2001, NN 6/A/2001 – Irish electricity out of peat.

82 Commission for Electricity Regulation (CER).

83 Commission, decision dated 13.12.2001, NN 6/A/2001, paras. 26–28 – Irish electricity out of peat.

84 *Heidenhain*, Verwendung des Aufkommens parafiskalischer Abgaben, EuZW 2005, 6; *Jaeger*, Beihilfen durch Steuern und parafiskalische Abgaben, (NWV Neuer Wiss. Verl., 2006), p. 300; *Meyer*, Die Bewertung parafiskalischer Abgaben aus der Sicht des europäischen Beihilferechts, (P. Lang), 2007, p. 141 f., who states, however, that requirements

coined in *Steinike* that had now become a widely spread formula[85] according to which Article 107(1) TFEU "*covers all aid granted by a Member State or through State resources without its being necessary to make a distinction whether the aid is granted directly by the State or by public or private bodies established or appointed by it to administer the aid.*"[86] In *PreussenElektra* it held: Article 107(1) "*is intended merely to bring within that definition both advantages which are granted directly by the State and those granted by a public or private body designated or established by the State.*"[87]

2. UK Renewables Obligation (November 2001)

Referring to *PreussenElektra*, the Commission held in November 2001 that two ways the UK Renewables Obligation could be fulfilled did not constitute aid: certificate purchase and a direct purchase of green energy did, according to the Commission, not involve State resources.[88] However, paying the buyout price (practically a fine for those who did not fulfill their obligation with energy or certificates) to a fund amounted to State aid because the Commission's three criteria test (see above 2.3.3) was fulfilled.[89]

3. Irish Renewable Energy Sources (January 2002)

Shortly after the first Irish case, in January 2002, the Commission took a more confident stand and held that the Irish Alternative Energy Requirement constituted

to establish State control have become more rigid; for a different opinion see *Soltész,* Die Entwicklung des europäischen Beihilferechts im Jahr 2013, EuZW 2011, 254, 256.

85 Case C-279/08 P *Commission/Netherlands (NOx emission trading)* [2011] ECR I-7471, para. 105; case C-222/07 *Unión de Televisiones Comerciales Asociadas (UTECA)/Administración General del Estado* [2009] ECR I-1407, para. 43; *Rusche/Micheau/Piffaut/van de Casteele,* State Aid, in: Faull/Nikpay (eds.): The EU law of competition, (OUP, 3rd ed. 2014), p. 1923 ff., para. 17.25.

86 Case 78/76 *Steinike & Weinlig* [1977] ECR 595, para. 21.

87 Case C-379/98 *PreussenElektra* [2001] ECR I-2099, para. 58.

88 Commission, decision dated 28.11.2001, N 504/2000, p. 10 ff. – United Kingdom Renewables Obligation.

89 Commission, decision dated 28.11.2001, N 504/2000, p. 12 f. – United Kingdom Renewables Obligation.

aid.[90] Its method of financing was essentially the same as in the peat promotion scheme.[91] This time, the Commission held:

> *"As the AER contracts were imposed on ESB by the Irish Government, it could be held that such contracts are similar to an obligation imposed on ESB by national law to purchase electricity from some Irish green electricity producers at a guaranteed price, and should, in application of the aforementioned Court ruling, be viewed as involving no State resources. […] However, the Commission notes that ESB is merely a vehicle for the distribution of the sums collected through the levy to AER contracts holders. One should therefore assess whether the transferred sums constitute State resources prior to their transit through ESB. […] According to constant practice of the Court, such sums constitute State resources in the meaning of Article 87(1) of the EC Treaty."*[92]

Here again, the three requirements mentioned above served the Commission as a benchmark for assessing the case: A levy had to be imposed by the State, the revenues were poured into an account controlled by the State or organisations established or designated by the State, and the funds were used to favour certain undertakings.[93] The Commission distinguished *PreussenElektra* from the earlier line of cases concerning parafiscal levies financing aid on the grounds that EBS simply served as a transit station for revenues that had already become State resources.[94] The argument of lacking corporate autonomy[95] regularly recurs in the CJEU's case law – e.g. in the form of designating a body as mere transit station or an instrument for implementing State policy.[96]

However, the Commission saw a potential conflict with Article 30 TFEU in the particular case where an electricity consumer would import all its electricity from

90 Commission, decision dated 15.1.2002, N 553/01 – Renewable Energy Sources in Ireland.

91 Commission, decision dated 15.1.2002, N 553/01, paras. 4–6 – Renewable Energy Sources in Ireland.

92 Commission, decision dated 15.1.2002, N 553/01, para. 12 – Renewable Energy Sources in Ireland.

93 Commission, decision dated 15.1.2002, N 553/01, para. 15 – Renewable Energy Sources in Ireland.

94 Commission, decision dated 15.1.2002, N 553/01, para. 13 – Renewable Energy Sources in Ireland.

95 *Bloch*, Die Befreiung von der EEG-Umlage als staatliche Beihilfe, RdE 2014, 14, 17 also elaborates on the antagonism of autonomy and control in determining whether a measure constitutes aid.

96 Case C-345/02 *Pearle* [2004] ECR I-7139, para. 37; case C-677/11 *Doux Élevages and Coopérative agricole UKL-AREE* EuZW 2011, 582, para. 40: "instruments".

other Member States.[97] In this situation the surplus charge would be paid for the consumption of imported energy alone. The Commission does not specifically express its concerns with regard to Article 30 TFEU as it is eager to state that this would remain for quite a while a purely hypothetical scenario – facing the low interconnection capacities between Ireland and its neighbouring countries. If we assumed that there were no or only minor congestions between Ireland and adjacent grids, the network charge in this particular "importer-scenario" would have constituted customs duty[98] and would have had to be abolished in order to be in line with Article 30 TFEU. Importers would have had to be exempted from the charge. If we, however, follow the Commission's assessment and Article 30 TFEU was out of the game due to "impossibility" of transmission, it is surprising how the Commission bypassed Article 110, which may nevertheless have applied.[99] It is surprising why its relevance should be prejudiced by low interconnection capacity, especially as neither Articles 30 and 110 nor Article 34 TFEU contain any threshold of appreciability.[100]

Any amount of electricity imported from another Member State finances EBS's losses. This money does not benefit any other undertaking than the contractual partners of EBS, who can assumed to be Irish. In later decisions concerning the Irish scheme the Commission developed a more stringent view of potentially discriminating collection modalities. In later decisions the Commission did not rescind this assessment of 2001 but recurred on the fact that the Renewables Obligation at least in part constituted aid to also review the amendments.[101]

---

97 Commission, decision dated 15.1.2002, N 553/01, para. 25 – Renewable Energies in Ireland.

98 Commission, decision dated 15.1.2002, N 553/01, para. 25 – Renewable Energies in Ireland: "In this case, although the levy would in principle not depend on the electricity consumption level, its practical effect would result in a charge imposed on imported electricity consumption".

99 The CJEU took this approach e.g. in *Essent Netwerk* (case C-206/06, ECR 2008, I-5497, paras. 47) and in case C-355/00 *Freskot* [2003] ECR I-5263, para. 40. It is not only the CJEUs constant practice to return to Article 110 once Article 30 has been refuted (or interpreted for the referring courts application) but mirrors the TFEU's systematic (see *Barnard*, The Substantive Law of the European Union. The Four Freedoms, (OUP, 4th ed. 2013), pp. 43 ff., 66 ff.).

100 Case C-206/06 *Essent Netwerk Noord* [2008] ECR I-5497, para. 76.

101 Commission, decision dated 29.7.2009, N 22/2009, para. 34 – United Kingdom Renewables Obligation – Northern Ireland; decision dated 11.2.2009, N 414/2008, para. 24 – UK Renewables Obligation – Introduction of a banding mechanism.

4. Green Certificates in Sweden (February 2002)

The national grid operator, Svenska Kraftnät, issued green certificates to operators of eligible plants. Consumers were to buy a fixed amount of certificates per Mwh. Suppliers were obliged to purchase the certificates for them and invoice a surcharge for the certificates and for their own administration charge. Non-compliant consumers and suppliers had to pay a fine feeding a special account administered by the Energy Agency. These monies were used to meet the expenses incurred by the guaranteed certificate prices. Similar to the UK Renewables Obligation case the Commission did not classify *the attribution of green certificates* to the plant operators by Svenska Kraftnät as aid because this action did not confer any benefit to the plant owners in the first place and could therefore not transfer State resources.[102]

Though the reasoning (focusing on losses to the State budget) is not totally convincing (plant operators could sell their certificates to consumers who had to fulfill a renewables quota) the General Court recurred on that argument. It firstly – obiter dictum – legitimated the Commission's assessment of green certificates in the Swedish case and secondly backed up its assessment with lacking budgetary losses.[103] However, the CJEU overturned the CFI and held that the attribution of free allowances, which could be sold on a market, constituted aid.[104] Apart from the certificate market the Commission considered – similar to the UK Renewables Obligation – the guaranteed price paid for green certificates from a fund fed with fines sufficient for transferring State resources.[105] Because the three afore mentioned criteria were fulfilled it qualified the financing mechanism as State aid.[106]

5. Austria – Support tariff for CHP (July 2006)

The Austrian support tariff for combined heat and power plants was partly financed by a surcharge collected by the grid operators from all network users. The charging rate corresponded with the surplus costs of financing electricity from

102 Commission, decision dated 5.2.2003, NN 789/2002, p. 4 f. – Green Certificates Sweden.

103 Case C-279/08 P *Commission/Netherlands (NOx emission trading)* [2011] ECR I-7471, para. 76.

104 Case C-279/08 P *Commission/Netherlands (NOx emission trading)* [2011] ECR I-7471, paras. 102 ff., esp. 111.

105 Commission, decision dated 5.2.2003, NN 789/2002, p. 5 – Green Certificates Sweden.

106 Commission, decision dated 5.2.2003, NN 789/2002, p. 4 – Green Certificates Sweden.

CHP. First the charge was levied according to consumption levels, then according to grid connection capacity.[107]

Let us first look at the State resources: The three criteria the Commission had developed earlier (that made the monies from the levy become State resources) were explicitly supplemented by a fourth criterion that the Commission took from the CJEU's *Pearle* judgment: Namely that the usage of the revenues had to be prescribed by the State as being earmarked for conferring a benefit on selected undertakings.[108] On the one hand it can be argued that already in *Italy/Commission* the Court demanded this obligatory link between charge and aid (hypothecation).[109]

On the other hand this fourth criterion clarifies the test and should, thus, be welcomed: It In fact it demands imputability to the State also in cases of parafiscal levies financing aid.[110] This allowed the Commission to more confidently State that the case law beginning with *Italy v. Commission* and *Steinike* was not altered by *PreussenElektra*.[111]

As the last interesting point the Commission noted that the old financing system based on a consumption levy did in fact discriminate against imported CHP electricity.[112] Though it does not specify the exact application of the mentioned Articles it is submitted here that Article 110(1) TFEU would have been the correct parameter.

6. Slovenia (April 2007)

Slovenian law allowed qualified plant operators to sell their electricity at a price above market level (which is set by the State) to their respective grid operator or demand a premium that covers the difference between the market revenue and the fixed price. This respective Commission decision deserves attention, because the Commission drew upon the arguments brought forward in the *Essent* judgment

107 Commission, decision dated 4.7.2006, NN 162/B/2003 and N 317/B/2006, para. 18 f. – Support tariff for CHP in Austria.

108 Commission, decision dated 4.7.2006, NN 162/B/2003 and N 317/B/2006, para. 37 – Support tariff for CHP in Austria.

109 Case 173/73 *Italy/Commission* [1974] ECR 709, para. 16: "they are managed and apportioned in accordance with the provisions of that legislation".

110 Commission, decision dated 4.7.2006, NN 162/B/2003 and N 317/B/2006, para. 37 – Support tariff for CHP in Austria.

111 Commission, decision dated 4.7.2006, NN 162/B/2003 and N 317/B/2006, para. 36 – Support tariff for CHP in Austria.

112 Commission, decision dated 4.7.2006, NN 162/B/2003 and N 317/B/2006, para. 42 f. and 53 f. – Support tariff for CHP in Austria.

(see 4. 2). According to the Commission, the Slovenian State exerts control over the funds – deciding whether charges should be paid, to what amount, and to what use they are put. Distinguishing the financing mechanism from *PreussenElektra* and the subsequent Commission decision on the German Renewable Energies Act 2000, the Commission recurred on the compulsive nature of the charges: Only the State would be in the position to levy undertakings.[113] The Commission also referred to the cases *Italy/Commission*, *Steinike* and the three prerequisites developed in its own earlier case-law.[114] To distinguish the system from the levy in the *Pearle* judgment, where payments rooted in a sector specific agreement of those who were charged with the extra fee, it stressed the initiative of the State and its power of implementation.

By now, the dichotomy of corporate freedom and State control is a well-known line of distinction between State policy and autonomous sector specific economic agreements.

More interestingly, the Commission also attached importance to the specific purpose of the charges: It suggested that charges collected from an industrial branch in order to directly benefit its members' economic activities (sector fees) may more readily be exempted from State aid law than "selfless" burdens the common electricity user is obliged to pay. In *Essent*, however, the CJEU stated that the identity and status of the burdened person were irrelevant,[115] but the Commission is right in one point: Chances are low that an autonomously acting undertaking would take the – economically unsound – decision to feed a fund that solely benefits others.

7. Luxembourg (January 2009)

Luxembourg legislation[116] imposed a purchase obligation for green electricity at a fixed price above market level on the general grid operator and after liberalization

113 Commission, decision dated 24.4.2007, C 7/2005, COM(2007) 1181 final, para. 73 – Slovenian producteurs d'énergie qualifiés: "Ce qui précède met en lumière la nature proprement fiscale d'un régime dont l'existence n'est possible qu'avec l'intervention de l'État."

114 Commission, decision dated 24.4.2007, C 7/2005, COM(2007) 1181 final, para. 73 – Slovenian producteurs d'énergie qualifies.

115 Case C-206/06 *Essent Netwerk Noord* [2008] ECR I-5497, paras. 48 f.

116 The promotion of renewable sources started with the so called Grand-Ducal Regulation in 1994 and was slightly altered in the years 2001, 2005, and 2009, see Commission, decision dated 28.1.2009, C 43/2002 ex NN 75/2001, paras. 15 ff. – Compensation fund for the organisation of the electricity market.

on all grid operators. Each distributor was authorised to collect charges from its consumers according to their electricity consumption (different categories of consumption defined the amount to be paid).[117] Functionally similar to the German Green Electricity Act, a fund was established by the State (a more detailed account of its operator were not given in the decision) to ensure that customers' burden would be proportionate to their electricity consumption. The legal obligation according to which distributors were to collect charges from their customers was only introduced in 2009 and not subject to the Commission's decision (which only covered the years up to 2008).[118]

The Commission assessed the monies as State resources and attributed the transfer decisions to the State because it was in control of the funds: It set the price for green electricity and decided upon the disbursement of the price surcharges. The Institut Luxembourgeois de Régulation (ILR) levelised the promotion costs between the distribution system operators who had to report their purchased amounts of green electricity and therefore exerted a good degree of control over the final charge. The operation of the fund turned private monies into State resources. As the Commission was eager to note, it was this and not the mere legal obligation to purchase green electricity at prices above market level.[119]

In the Luxembourg case the Commission demanded a mechanism to be set up to compensate those consumers who had purchased green electricity from abroad. Otherwise the system would have discriminated against foreign green electricity, which was levied but did not profit from the money in the fund. Again, the Commission did not engage in detailed legal analysis whether Article 30 or 110 TFEU would have been applicable. Requiring the removal of the discriminating element, however, allows the conclusion that the Commission considered Art. 110 TFEU to be applicable.

8. UK FIT (2010)

The feed-in tariff system for small scale renewable energy plants that the UK notified with the Commission in 2010 imposed on solely privately owned suppliers

117 Commission, decision dated 28.1.2009, C 43/2002 ex NN 75/2001, paras. 20 and 22 – Compensation fund for the organisation of the electricity market.

118 This question would have been of particular interest since it mirrors the type of obligation in § 37(2) German Renewable Energy Act 2012 and § 60(1) EEG.

119 Commission, decision dated 28.1.2009, C 43/2002 ex NN 75/2001, para. 28 – Compensation fund for the organisation of the electricity market.

the obligation to pay feed-in tariffs to certain RES-E plants.[120] The suppliers were burdened with the costs according to their market share. To ensure this allocation a levelisation mechanism was put in place according to which suppliers had to pay or withdraw money from a fund in order to arrive at their respective shares. Suppliers, however, had to deduct from their FIT balance amounts of green energy they had imported.[121] This way, those quantities of imported renewable electricity did not participate in the cost bearing mechanism and a conflict with Articles 30 and 110 TFEU was avoided.

9. Preliminary conclusion

In the Commission's case-law we can track the disruption *PreussenElektra* has caused in the State aid assessment of renewable promotion schemes. In early cases the Commission struggled to ascertain the judgment's appropriate scope and assessed elements differently that were part of one promotion scheme with one single objective (UK Renewables Obligation, see C. II.). Once the Commission resorted to the line of cases dealing with parafiscal levies it took a more confident stand on the assessment of promotion schemes. The free disbursement of allowances that plant operators could subsequently sell on a market would today be qualified as aid.[122] Since the *PreussenElektra* case the CJEU has also significantly developed its case-law on the State test and its application to the energy sector. Two cases, *Essent Netwerk Noord* and *Vent De Colère!* shall be singled out and examined further in the following section.

IV. The Recent Judgments of *Essent Netwerk* and *Vent de Colère!*

1. *Essent Netwerk*

In *Essent Netwerk*[123] the CJEU issued a preliminary ruling concerning a system to defray stranded costs that selected undertakings had incurred before the market liberalisation under the first Electricity Market Directive 96/92/EG. Network operators (such as *Essent Netwerk*) had to collect a surcharge from every customer in accordance to the amount of transmitted energy. A ministerial order set the level

120 Commission, decision dated 14.4.2010, N 94/2010, para. 15 – UK Feed In Tariffs.

121 Commission, decision dated 14.4.2010, N 94/2010, para. 46 – UK Feed In Tariffs.

122 Case C-279/08 P *Commission/Netherlands (NOx emission trading)* [2011] ECR I-7471.

123 Case C-206/06 *Essent Netwerk Noord* [2008] ECR I-5497.

of the charge. The grid operator channeled the money to SEP who, again, conferred it to the selected undertakings. SEP was owned by several public undertakings and therefore controlled by State.[124]

2. *Essent's* contribution to the State test

Essent Netwerk contributes to the understanding of the State test in one important way: It presents what can be called a "missing link" between the State test in Article 107(1) and Articles 30 and 110 TFEU. Namely, once an aid measure is financed through mandatory surcharges in the sense of Articles 30 and 110 TFEU those are through their nature as public levies regarded as State resources:

> "*In that regard, it must be borne in mind that those amounts have their origin in the price surcharge imposed by the State on purchasers of electricity [...], a surcharge with regard to which it has been established, in paragraph 47 of this judgment, that it constitutes a charge. Those amounts thus have their origin in a State resource.*"[125]

A weakness of the judgment lies in the lack of reliable distinction between State resources on the one hand and the involvement of the State in the decision to transfer money on the other.[126] After the above cited passage the Court, nevertheless, further elaborates on the question of State resources in paras. 70–74. Cited passages of case law also without exception deal with the imputability of private resources to the sphere of the State – including the *Stardust Marine*[127] case, which was not cited for its list of indicators for State involvement but its assessment of State resources.[128]

---

124 Within the meaning of the second indent of the first subparagraph of Article 2 of Commission Directive 80/723/EEC of 25 June 1980 on the transparency of financial relations between Member States and public undertakings (OJ 1980 L 195, p. 35).

125 Case C-206/06 *Essent Netwerk Noord* [2008] ECR I-5497, para. 66.

126 At the beginning of the *Essent* judgement (para. 65) the Court sets out to examine "whether the amounts paid to SEP constitute intervention by the State *or* through State resources" (emphasis added) only to conclude at the end (para. 75): "It follows from all of those points that the amounts paid to SEP constitute intervention by the State through State resources".

127 Case C-482/99 *France/Commission (Stardust Marine)* [2002] ECR I-4397.

128 Those can be found in case C-482/99 *France/Commission (Stardust Marine)* [2002] ECR I-4397, paras. 50 to55.

3. *Vent de Colère!*

The Association *Vent De Colère!* challenged two French regulations that amplified a purchase obligation of electricity from wind-power.[129] French suppliers had to purchase this green electricity at a fixed price above market level (Art. 8 and 10 of the Law No 2008–108) and were reimbursed for the additional costs by the Caisse des dépôts et consignations on a quarterly basis. The Caisse is a public law corporation the personnel of which are largely appointed by Governmental institutions and regularly either belong to the Senate or the French Chamber of Deputies.

The credit institute manages a separate account with proceeds from a network surcharge that system operators collected from end consumers. Their charge is usage-bound and covers the additional costs for wind energy as well as the administration costs of the Caisse that were set by ministerial order every year. The French State agreed to set off costs that could not be covered by the proceeds.[130]

4. *Vent de Colère's* importance for the State test

Twelve years after *PreussenElektra* the *Vent De Colère!* judgment is the second landmark ruling on State aid assessment of renewable energy purchase obligations. Since 2001 the CJEU has substantially developed its case-law concerning State involvement: A year after *PreussenElektra Stardust Marine* was handed down and could now be accounted for in *Vent De Colère!*. In fact, it was the first time the CJEU explicitly and comprehensively applied the *Stardust* control test[131] to an aid scheme in the energy sector.

In *Freskot* the Court already declared the Stardust test applicable to systems of parafiscal levies – but only obiter dictum.[132] In *Pearle*[133] the Court also recurred on *Stardust* but its concrete scope remained blurry. Only recently, in *Doux Élevages*, the Court thoroughly applied the list of criteria explicitly to an aid system.[134]

In contrast to the *Essent* judgment the CJEU in *Vent De Colère!* clearly distinguished between the State's involvement in the transfer decision and its control of the resources. The control over the transfer decision the CJEU shortly assumed

---

129 Case C-262/12 *Vent De Colère!* EuZW 2014, p. 115.

130 Case C-262/12 *Vent De Colère!* EuZW 2014, p. 115, para. 26.

131 The heart of it is found in Case C-482/99 *France/Commission (Stardust Marine)* [2002] ECR I-4397, paras. 55 to 57.

132 Case C-355/00 *Freskot* [2003] ECR I-5263, para. 103.

133 Case C-345/02 *Pearle* [2004] ECR I-7139, para. 54.

134 Case C-677/11 *Doux Élevages and Coopérative agricole UKL-AREE* EuZW 2011, 582, paras. 34–36.

by recurring on the obligatory nature of the Law No 2008–108.[135] Whereas this argument was used in *Essent* to establish State resources it is now used to demonstrate control over the transfer decision. From that we can conclude that the obligatory nature of the law plays an important role in assessing whether the State controlled the funds and the transfer decision. But it also shows that control cannot be established abstractly – as the Court clarified in *Stardust Marine* – but has to be found only after analysing the concrete legal framework.

Private payments from end consumers became State resources because the Caisse as a public body under State mandate had reporting duties to the French regulatory authority, invoiced late payments and administrative penalties and thus controlled the means.[136] The CJEU assesses the degree of public control by applying the different control criteria to the legislative framework that sets up the financing mechanism. Apart from the operation of the Caisse, the rate of the charges, the purpose for which they will be used, and the administrative supervision – all core elements of the financing mechanism – are laid down in Law No 2008–108 or amplifying Ministerial Orders. This perception of control is supported by the grounds for distinguishing *PreussenElektra*[137] from the *Vent De Colère!* case: The old German Renewable Energies Obligation was based on few provisions and did not regulate in detail any administrative enforcement; instead parties had to resort to private law enforcement. The legislative framework in *PreussenElektra* was not as sophisticated and refined as it is in most offsetting mechanisms today.[138]

V. Conclusion

Art. 108 TFEU provides the Commission with a useful and highly needed tool to foster the further development of the internal energy market. By reviewing fiscal measures that finance RES support systems in the State aid procedure the

---

135 Case C-262/12 *Vent De Colère!* EuZW 2014, 115, para. 18.

136 Case C-262/12 *Vent De Colère!* EuZW 2014, 115, paras. 29–30.

137 Court and Commission have consequently distinguished *PreussenElektra* and diminished its impact. Though not in the energy sector, the single exception to this shall not be omitted: case C-222/07 *Unión de Televisiones Comerciales Asociadas (UTECA)/ Administración General del Estado* [2009] ECR I-1407.

138 Case C-262/12 *Vent De Colère!* EuZW 2014, 115, para. 34: "All those factors taken together serve to distinguish the present case from that which gave rise to the judgment in PreussenElektra."

Commission can comprehensively oversee Member States' renewable promotion policies.

After some teething troubles in earlier decisions the Commission would order Member States to not impose a surcharge on imported green electricity. That the Commission did not require the German authorities to compensate for past discrimination in the EEG 2012 and the EEG 2014 schemes[139] seems to be at odds with its earlier decisions in the area of renewable energy promotion.

Essent Netwerk is a remarkable case because it illustrates how provisions on financial charges (Articles 30 and 110 TFEU) interact with the notion of State aid: With its character as a charge the Court assumes the State origin of its proceeds. While in *Essent* the Court does not readily distinguish between the two elements of the State test – namely the involvement in the aid decision and the origin of the resources – it clarifies these two elements in the subsequent case of *Vent De Colère!*. Here, the CJEU in an exemplary fashion engages in the State test and comprehensively applies the framework laid down in *Stardust Marine* to the provisions setting up the financing mechanism. The *Stardust* indicators may, thus, be applied just as effectively to a legislative framework as to individual aid measures.

139 Commission, decision dated 23.7.2014, SA.38632, paras. 329 ff. – EEG 2014; Commission, decision dated 25.11.2014, SA.33995, para. 243 – EEG 2012.

Lydia Scholz
Professor of Law
City University of Applied Sciences Bremen
lydia.scholz@hs-bremen.de

The dialogue between the principle of free movement of goods and the national law of renewable energies

Content

I. Introduction

The European Union obliges Member States to promote the use of renewable energies by Article 3 of the RES Directive. The Member States have therefore implemented national promotion schemes, either feed-in schemes or quota obligation and certificate schemes.[1] Both types usually come with a limited scope of application only covering electricity production in the State's own territory.

Setting out such territorial limitations excludes the promotion of non-domestic electricity which can restrict trade on electricity within the meaning of Article 34 of the TFEU in a discriminatory manner.

The German feed-in system as well as the Swedish-Norwegian and the Flemish quota obligation and certificate system have challenged the Court of Justice of the European Union (Court) to assess possible justifications for those discriminatory regimes which aim to protect the environment. In 2001, the Court gave its *PreussenElektra* judgment[2] on the basis of the German scheme. More than a decade later, in 2014, the *Ålands Vindkraft* judgment[3] was given with reference to the Swedish-Norwegian Scheme as well as the *Essent Belgium* judgment[4] with regard to the Flemish scheme. In these three rulings the Court contributed to legal certainty by stating that national promotion schemes attaining the objective of environmental protection do not infringe the fundamental principle of free movement of goods despite their discriminatory character.

This outcome, however, is not in line with the conventional concept of justification. National renewable energy promotion schemes thus forced the Court and legal scholars to rethink the traditional concept of free movement of goods and its grounds for justification. This paper attempts to reconstruct the concept of justification on the basis of the aforementioned three judgments.

First, the impact of territoriality clauses in national promotion schemes is outlined. This is followed by an assessment of the trade restrictions under the traditional justification scheme.

Thirdly, the reasoning of the Court in *PreussenElektra*, *Ålands Vindkraft* and *Essent Belgium* will be analysed. Finally, on this basis, an attempt will be made to draw a new picture of the grounds for justification.

---

1 *Säcker/König/Scholz*, Der regulierungsrechtliche Rahmen für ein Offshore-Stromnetz in der Nordsee, 2014, p. 104 ff., 167, 168.

2 C-379/98 *PreussenElektra* [2001] ECR I-2099.

3 C-573/12 *Ålands Vindkraft*, not yet reported, para. 12.

4 C-204/12 to 208/12 *Essent Belgium*, not yet reported, para. 89.

II. Territoriality clauses within national promotion systems

National promotion systems are respectively limited in their territorial scope to the territory of that State whose legislative body they were issued by.

1. Examples from national renewable energy laws

In Germany the territorial scope of the Renewable Energies Act (EEG) is defined in the Act itself. § 4 EEG thus defines its scope as the federal territory "including the German exclusive economic zone". From an international law perspective the wording is rather unfortunate due to the fact that a State's territory precisely does not include its exclusive economic zone (EEZ). According to § 4 EEG the Act merely applies to plants within the territory of the Federal Republic of Germany or within the German EEZ, whereas it does not to plants located abroad.

As such the operator of e.g. a wind energy plant situated on the Dutch side of the German-Dutch border is not able to bring a valid action against a German network operator under the EEG, if the German incentive system seems to him to be more attractive than the Dutch one. Even in the case of plants situated abroad, yet connected to the network of a German network operator due to e.g. technical or historical reasons, it is not possible to bring a claim under the EEG.

Similar provisions can be found under Danish and Dutch law.[5] § 3(1) VE-Lov limits any form of promotion to plant locations within Denmark, their territorial waters as well as the Danish EEZ. Under Dutch law such promotion is limited to plant locations situated within Dutch territory and their EEZ according to Article 1(1m) SDE+ in conjunction with section 2 of the Dutch Territoriality Act. In a similar vein, Article 1 des Arrêté du 17 novembre 2008 limits the French promotion system to the territory of France and its EEZ.

Likewise the United Kingdom has made their promoting of renewable energy systems dependent on the plants' site location. In the case of e.g. offshore installations this is a consequence of examining two separate provisions. On the one hand, the territorial limits to a promotion system can in part be deduced from the definition of offshore waters in section 2 Renewables Obligation Order (ROO)[6], according to which offshore waters are those which either lie within the United Kingdom itself or have been assigned to it and lie in between the low-water line and the seaward limit of the UK's territorial sea as well as waters situated within

---

5 See *Säcker/König/Scholz*, Der regulierungsrechtliche Rahmen für ein Offshore-Stromnetz in der Nordsee, (P. Lang, 2014), p. 114.

6 Renewables Obligation Order 2009 for England and Wales.

an area which has been demarcated according to section 1(7) of the Continental Shelf Act, thus the 200 nautical mile zone.

On the other hand, section 1(7) ROO excludes promoting, i.e. allocating certificates to, those plants located beyond the seaward limit of the territorial waters ascribed to the United Kingdom unless these plants are located in one of the zones laid out in section 1(7) Continental Shelf Act or within a renewable energies zone.

As from 1 January 2012 Sweden has set up a common quota-certificate system with Norway with a scope of application also limited to the relevant national territories. For Norway the legal basis is the Electricity Certificates Act and the Electricity Certificates Regulation *(Forskrift om elsertifikater)*, for Sweden it is the *Lag om elcertifikat* (2011:1200). According to Chapter 4 §§ 1 et seq. of the Swedish Lag om elcertifikat (2011:1200) electricity suppliers, registered electricity-intensive companies as well as particular consumer groups are under an obligation to present a certificate of origin for a set proportion of their energy mix. These certificates are granted in accordance with the provisions in Chapter 2 of the *Lag om elcertifikat* (2011:1200) for the generation of electricity from renewable energy sources.

The value of a certificate is equivalent to one MWh of the electricity produced. Chapter 6 § 1 of the *Lag om elcertifikat* (2011:1200) lays out a penalty mechanism/mechanism of sanctions in order to ensure the obligations under Chapter 4 are adhered to. Should an addressee of this provision be unable to present the respective certificate of origin they then incur a fine of 150 % of the average certificate value. In Sweden and Norway the certificates are granted by the respective national authorities for the generation of electricity within their own national territory.

The joint element of both systems is that certificates can be traded in the territories of both States and that these then serve as evidence to one another of generating electricity from renewable energy sources. Even though both countries do not necessarily limit such promotion to production processes within their own respective national territory, they do nevertheless exclude plants located outside Sweden and Norway as it follows from the legislative preparatory works.[7]

Other States, too, solely promote plants within their own territory with their respective systems of economic incentives although they are not actually obliged to do so under international law. Whilst the territoriality principle under international law does prohibit extending obligations to another country's sovereign territory it does not do so when it comes to granting certain advantages for cases outside one's own sovereign territory. Rather, setting out territorial limitations

---

7 C-573/12 *Ålands Vindkraft*, not reported yet, para. 12.

on promotion systems is in fact either due to reasons of budgetary and industrial policy or can be seen as a consequence of restrictive criteria of application which merely allow for domestic plants to be recipients of such promotion.

2. Territoriality clauses in light of the free movement of goods

European Union law, which has committed itself to the achievement of the internal market by way of the free movement of goods amongst other things, is constructed in such a way so as to limit the way in which certain forms of protectionism exhibited by territoriality clauses are able to take effect.

This fundamental prohibition of protectionist policies applies not only to all 28 EU Member States but also to Norway, by virtue of Article 7 of the Agreement on the Economic Area (EEA).[8] Norway has been part of the EEA since 1 January 1994 and thereby also partakes of the EU's internal market. As such, Norway is under an obligation to implement the *acquis communautaire* insofar as the relevant legal act which is to be implemented has formally been incorporated in the EEA agreement. As a rule all legal acts relevant to the internal market are incorporated in such a way, especially ones relevant to primary EU law, but also all acts of secondary legislation relating to European energy law.

National promotion systems are still to be assessed in relation to Article 34 TFEU and the principle of free movement of goods rooted therein.[9] The fact that the EU has put Member States under an obligation to implement national promotion systems by virtue of Article 3 of the RES Directive, has not altered this. *Advocate General Bot* regarded this provision as exhaustive harmonisation and as a *carte blanche* for the exclusion of plants outside a State's respective sovereign territory.[10] It is settled case law that a national provision is not to be assessed in light of the Treaties if it falls into an area already exhaustively harmonised at Union level.[11] In this case the national provision is to be examined in light of the relevant

8 Agreement on the European Economic Area, OJ 1994 L 1/3.

9 See also *von Unger*, Germany's renewable Energy Law, State Aid and the Internal Market, Journal for European Environmental & Planning Law, 117, 130, 131.

10 AG Bot in Joined Cases C-204/12–208/12 *Essent Belgium*, not yet reported, paras. 78 ff. See also *Kröger*, Nationally Exclusive Support Schemes for RES Electricity Production and the Free Movement of Goods, Journal for European Environmental & Planning Law, 10.4 (2013), 378, 382 ff.

11 C-37/92 *Vanacker and Lesage*, [1993] ECR, I-4947, para. 9; C-324/99 *DaimlerChrysler*, [2001] ECR, I-9897, para. 32; C-322/01 *DocMorris*, [2003] ECR, I-14887, para. 64; C-309/02 *Radlberger*, [2004] ECR, I-11763, para. 53.

harmonisation measure under secondary legislation.[12] However, the promotion of renewable energy sources has not yet been exhaustively harmonised. Article 3 of the RES Directive allows for Member States to enjoy considerable leeway with regard to implementation during which they are, of course, obliged to adhere to primary European law and as such to the principle of free movement of goods.

a) *Electricity as a good*

The Court, in its line of established case law, has accorded electricity the quality of a good and, as a consequence thereof, national systems which promote the generation of electricity from renewable energy sources have to withstand scrutiny under the principle of free movement of goods.[13]

b) *Negative impact on trade*

Due to the fact that the applicability of a national promotion system is limited to the production process within the territory of the relevant Member State, such national measures have the ability to affect the trade of electricity between these States, thereby fulfilling the requirements set out by the Court in order to establish a measure having equivalent effect to a quantitative restriction on imports. As a result of territoriality clauses, only domestic electricity is able to benefit from such a promotion system. In as early as its *Du Pont de Nemours Italiana* judgment the Court considered the *Dassonville* requirements fulfilled in such circumstances.[14] So too, the national promotion systems' advantageous effect on domestic electricity production constitutes a measure having equivalent effect, with reference to *Prantl*. Here the Court set out that national legal provisions constitute measures having equivalent effect if their practical impact is such as to protect (typically) domestic production, not only through the direct award of benefits but also by correspondingly placing certain types of products from other Member States at a disadvantage.[15]

The Court specifically confirmed the German feed-in system of having a restrictive effect on trade in its *PreussenElektra* judgment. Having ascertained the

12 C-37/92 *Vanacker and Lesage*, [1993] ECR, I-4947, para. 9; C-324/99 *DaimlerChrysler*, [2001] ECR, I-9897, para. 32; C-322/01 *DocMorris*, [2003] ECR, I-14887, para. 64; C-309/02 *Radlberger*, [2004] ECR, I-11763, para. 53.

13 C-393/92 *Almelo*, [1994] ECR, I-1477, para. 28; C-379/98 *PreussenElektra* [2001] ECR I-2099, paras. 68 ff.; C-573/12 *Ålands Vindkraft*, not yet reported, paras. 56 ff.

14 C-21/88 *Du Pont de Nemours Italiana*, [1990] ECR, I-889, para. 13.

15 C-16/83 *Prantl*, [1984] ECR, I-1299, para. 21.

particularities as well as the effects the purchase and payment obligations under the German Stromeinspeisungsgesetz (Electricity Feeding Act) had, the Court reached the conclusion that these were indeed capable of potentially hindering intra-Union trade.[16]

III. Promotion schemes under traditional justification schemes

In both feed-in systems as well as quota obligation and certificate systems territoriality clauses lead to intra-Union trade in electricity being restricted in a discriminatory way within the meaning of the *Dassonville* formula. As such, the question of a possible justification remains. When considering the feature common amongst all existing systems promoting renewable energy sources, which can be described as discriminatory State measures for protecting the environment, the following picture emerges, in accordance with the textbook definition of legal doctrine on the criteria for such justification within the internal market.

1. Justification under Article 36 TFEU

While Article 36 TFEU expressly provides for certain justifications of an infringement of the free movement of goods its scope merely includes discriminatory State measures with certain objectives, of which environmental protection is not one. Article 36(1) TFEU does not explicitly list protecting the environment as a possible justification, nor can this be included in aiming to "protect human, animal or plant life and health" as this would require the respective national measure to directly and specifically protect health and life.[17]

Undoubtedly, national promotion systems directly and specifically aim to protect the environment. However, they only do so indirectly when it comes to protecting human, animal or plant life and health. The list of justifications provided by Article 36 TFEU is exhaustive and as such Article 36(1) TFEU cannot be interpreted in such a way as to include environmental protection within its wording. National promotion schemes can therefore not be justified under Article 36 TFEU.

2. Justification under the *Cassis* formula

The Court had perceived that the fact that Member States had further good reasons for enacting certain State measures, more than were provided for by Article 36 TFEU, was worth recognising as early as the 1970s.

---

16 C-379/98 *PreussenElektra* [2001] ECR I-2099, paras. 70 f.

17 See the ruling of C-113/80 *Irish Souvenirs*, [1981] ECR, I-1625, paras. 7 f.

In its famous *Cassis* judgment the Court laid out a formula aimed at enabling State measures which had an impairing effect on the internal market to comply with European law.[18] The Court refers to this formula assiduously in its judgments, having extended it by a variety of mandatory requirements. Hereby, the Court used to require the relevant measure be of an *indiscriminate* nature.[19] It is for this reason that the traditional *Cassis* formula, too, is unsuitable for bringing about the conformity of promotion systems with European law, due to the fact that territoriality clauses by virtue of their discriminatory nature precisely do not have the required indiscriminate effect. Therefore the question arises as to how the Court has been able to justify promotion systems which are national in their scope.

IV. Justification of national promotion schemes in the case-law

1. The *PreussenElektra* judgment

The Court first considered the issue of the admissibility under European Union law of territoriality clauses within a national promotion system in its *PreussenElektra* judgment.[20] The basis for this judgment from 2001 was the promotion system established by the *Stromeinspeisegesetz* (the German Electricity Feeding Act) which was the current system's predecessor. However, the Court's reasoning in the judgment's passage on the justification of territoriality clauses posed more questions than it answered in relation to the construct of the free movement of goods.

Ultimately, the protection of the environment as a form of justification, entirely separate from those provided by Article 36(1) TFEU or the *Cassis* formula and its ensuing case law, was considered.[21] This line of reasoning seemed to stem from a comprehensive examination in which the balance between both Treaty objectives – free movement of goods on the one hand and environmental protection on the other – is assessed.[22] This includes gauging to what extent these objectives can be subject to certain limitations as well as weighing them up against each other so that both may achieve their maximum efficacy in relation to each other. Depending on the specific facts of each case it is thus to be determined whether the right balance between the principle of free movement of goods and the

---

18 C-120/78 *Cassis de Dijon*, [1979] ECR, 649, para. 8.

19 *Scholz*, Die Rechtfertigung von diskriminierenden umweltpolitischen Steuerungsinstrumenten, (P. Lang 2012), p. 177 ff.

20 C-379/98 *PreussenElektra* [2001] ECR I-2099, paras. 70 ff.

21 C-379/98 *PreussenElektra* [2001] ECR I-2099, paras. 70, 72.

22 *Scholz*, Die Rechtfertigung von diskriminierenden umweltpolitischen Steuerungsinstrumenten, (P. Lang, 2012), p. 201 ff.

protection of the environment has been struck.[23] Factors such as promotion systems' environmentally protective effects and the extent to which systems infringe upon the free movement of goods are to be considered in the process.[24]

a) *Relevance of environmentally protective impact*

Whether a justification can take full effect or is of merely limited use is essentially determined by certain requirements which the environmentally protective impact of promotion systems has to provide. Their objective is protecting the environment. Environmental protection requirements are set out in Article 11 TFEU as well as Article 6(1) TEU in conjunction with Article 37 of the Union's Charter of Fundamental Rights and they are substantiated by Article 191 TFEU. Article 191(1) TFEU requires the objective of a national measure to be in pursuit of one of the following: preserving, protecting and improving the quality of the environment, protecting human health, prudent and rational utilisation of natural resources or promoting measures at international level to deal with environmental problems. Consideration can be given to whether national systems promoting renewable energy sources are either in pursuit of the preservation, protection and improvement of the quality of the environment or have determined the prudent and rational utilisation of natural resources as their objective.

b) *Intensity of the impediment of the free movement of goods*

The intensity with which the principle of free movement of goods is infringed upon is to be judged in light of both qualitative and quantitative terms. With reference to qualitative characteristics it should be taken into consideration that, given the territoriality clauses, promotion systems constitute instruments that do not actually or directly hinder intra-Union trade, but do so merely potentially or indirectly. As a rule, indirect and potential effects on trade are rarely quantifiable. Quite possibly, it is for this reason the Court does not consider the quantitative degree of trade impact in the context of free movement of goods.

c) *Principle of "praktische Konkordanz"*

National promotion schemes, even though they infringe upon intra-Union trade and, thus, upon the free movement of goods, take into account the requirements

---

23 C-379/98 *PreussenElektra* [2001] ECR I-2099, para. 73.

24 *Scholz*, Die Rechtfertigung von diskriminierenden umweltpolitischen Steuerungsinstrumenten, (P. Lang, 2012), p. 193 ff.

of environmental protection, in particular with a view to promoting sustainable development, thereby meeting the Union's environmental requirements set out in Article 11 TFEU as well as Article 6(1) TEU in conjunction with Article 37 of the Charter of Fundamental Rights. As such, the objectives of free movement of goods and environmental protection, both equally important in primary Union law, collide. Such a collision can be resolved by means of a comprehensive analysis in accordance with the principle of "*praktische Konkordanz*".

This method is known from French and German constitutional law and consists of weighing up objectives of the constitution against each other which are of equal value so that both may achieve their maximum efficacy in relation to each other. In national constitutional law fundamental rights, for example, are of same value.

If a State's measure infringes a fundamental right for the benefit of another fundamental right, both can be weighted up against each other with the effect that the State's infringement of that fundamental right can be justified. In EU law, the objectives of the EU, for example, are of same value.

National promotion schemes have an effect on both the environment and the internal market. In weighting up those effects against each other, due regard is to be given to the fact that the national promotion mechanisms take environmental protection into account, in actual fact and in a quantifiable manner. Furthermore, any effects in qualitative terms, which these environmentally protective mechanisms have on the free movement of goods, are to be taken into consideration. Free movement would not be infringed upon if national promotion schemes were extended to electricity produced in other Member States. Expanding the scope of promotion legislation to this extent would not necessarily give rise to negative effects on the protection of the environment. Limiting the scope of these regulations to production processes within a country's national territory is not in itself a necessary precaution in order to reduce greenhouse gas emissions and achieve environmental protection.

This justification is not rendered unworkable by the fact that the *Cassis* formula merely applies to indiscriminately applicable measures. Rather, the principle of practical concordance, the application of which is attributable to the fact that the objectives of free movement of goods and environmental protection are of equal standing, allows for this justification to also apply to discriminatory measures.

With regard to the quantitative effects promotion mechanisms have on the free movement of goods, it is necessary to bear in mind that a steadily growing environmentally protective impact is accompanied by a similar increase in market foreclosure and thus by a greater infringement of the free movement of goods. The practical effect of the free movement of goods means that in quantitative terms the appreciability requirement of Article 101(1) TFEU in conjunction with the *de minimis* notice[25] should be observed. Any foreclosure of the market extending beyond the threshold of appreciability is – by virtue of the analogous application of competition law – incompatible with the internal market, even with a holistic one.

Otherwise, competition law and the free movement of goods would, in quantitative terms, manifest themselves in different ways within the internal market, consequently bringing about a distortion of its principles. While the intensity with which free movement of goods has been infringed upon has largely remained unaltered since the promotion of the generation of electricity from renewable energy sources began, it has, however, significantly changed in quantitative terms. The Court's *PreussenElektra* judgment from 2001 was based on the fact that the German renewable energy promotion scheme caused a market foreclosure of one percent of electricity consumption.[26]

The actual basis of calculation for this figure cannot be gleaned from either the Opinion of the Advocate General nor the judgment itself. According to information provided by the Federal Ministry for the Environment, Nature Conservation and Nuclear Safety the share of domestic electricity consumption in 2000 in fact amounted to 6.4 percent.[27]

By way of contrast, in 2010, the share of renewable energies reached 16.8 percent of total domestic electricity consumption, thereby rising by 3.1 percent compared to the previous year.[28] In 2010, around 80 percent of this type of renewable electricity gained access to the German electricity market due to the EEG's purchase and payment instrument. This, in turn, constitutes a share of around 13.4 percent of renewable energies in electricity consumption in 2010.

Pursuant to § 1(2) EEG the percentage of renewable energies contributing to the electricity supply is to be increased to 80 percent by 2050. It is the aforementioned percentages which reflect the scope of potential market foreclosure, a result the EEG and its promotion mechanisms did certainly not intend but which will inevitably arise. In 2010, the German electricity market was potentially foreclosed to market entry by around 13.4 percent. Such potential market foreclosure will

---

25 Commission Notice on agreements of minor importance which do not appreciably restrict competition under Article 101(1) of the TFEU.

26 AG Jacobs, C-379/98 *PreussenElektra*, [2001] ECR 2099, para. 203.

27 *Scholz*, Die Rechtfertigung von diskriminierenden umweltpolitischen Steuerungsinstrumenten, (P. Lang, 2012), p. 253 f.

28 For further references see *Scholz*, Die Rechtfertigung von diskriminierenden umweltpolitischen Steuerungsinstrumenten, (P. Lang, 2012), p. 253 f.

increase in correlation with the political aims of expanding renewable energies. This will limit the practical effects of the principle of free movement of goods.

2. The *Ålands Vindkraft* judgment

More than one decade later the Court again ruled on the compatibility of a national promotion scheme with the principle of free movement of goods. This judgment was based on the Swedish-Norwegian support scheme which is a quota obligation and certificate scheme. It derived from the preparatory works that certificated are only awarded to green electricity production installations to Sweden[29] and Norway. The scheme is therefore of a discriminatory character.

Having outlined the barriers to trade caused by the design of the Swedish-Norwegian scheme, the Court referred to its previous case law and Stated that measures having an equivalent effect to quantitative restrictions might be justified on one of the public grounds listed in Article 36 TFEU or by overriding requirements.[30] Without reference to one of these alternatives, the court highlighted that the national promotion scheme must be appropriate for the ensuring attainment of the protection of the objective pursued and must not go beyond what is necessary in order to attain that objective.[31] This was followed by an assessment of the objective of the promotion scheme – being environmental protection[32] and by a detailed assessment of the proportionality.[33]

The Court then concluded that the principle of free movement of goods does not preclude national legislation promoting the use of renewable energies by awarding certificated only to green electricity producers in respect to green electricity only produced in the territory of the relevant Member State. In the end, the Court again justified a national discriminatory measure with the objective of environmental protection.

3. The *Essent Belgium* judgment

The Court thirdly considered the compliance of national discriminatory promotion schemes in its *Essent Belgium* judgment. The basis for this judgment from 2014 was the Flemish quota obligation and certificate promotion system established

29 C-573/12 *Ålands Vindkraft*, not yet reported, para. 12.
30 Ibid., para. 76.
31 Ibid., para. 76.
32 Ibid., paras. 77 to 82.
33 Ibid., paras. 83 to 118.

by the *Vlaams decreet houdende de organisatie van de elektriciteitmarkt* (the Flemish Decree on the organisation of the electricity market).

According to Article 22 of that decree it is provided that certificates will be issued for electricity produced in the Flemish region which causes discrimination of non-domestic electricity.

The Court referred to the *Ålands Vindkraft* judgment and stated that national legislation that constitutes a measure having an equivalent effect to quantitative restrictions might be justified on one of the public grounds listed in Article 36 TFEU or by overriding requirements.[34] In either case, the Court continued, the national promotion scheme must be appropriate for the ensuring attainment of the protection of the environment being the objective and must not go beyond what is necessary in order to attain that objective.[35]

On this basis the court assessed the objective of promoting renewable energy sources[36] and deeply the proportionality.[37] This finally led to the conclusion that the discriminatory Flemish promotion scheme was justified. In contrast to *PreussenElektra* the Court expressively mentioned the legal grounds for justification – Article 36 TFEU and overriding requirements which have been developed under the *Cassis* formula. However, it did not state which one of these two grounds for justification was applied. The question remains if and to what extent the justification of measures having an equivalent effect as quantitative restriction have been changed.

V. Reconstruction of the principle of free movement of goods

In light of the case law presented so far, it can be stated that the principle of free movement of goods in Article 34 TFEU does not exclude national discriminatory measures which are aimed at the protection of the environment. It is obvious that the series of cases dealing with national renewable energy promotion schemes has fundamentally changed the concept of justification applicable to free movement of goods. Although it was arguable after the *PreussenElektra* ruling that the Court applied a new type of justification different to that of Article 36 TFEU and that of the *Cassis* formula, which allows a justification of discriminatory national measures aimed at the protection of the environment on the basis of balancing the interest of equal value – a method known from German and French constitutional

---

34 Joint cases C-204/12 to 208/12, *Essent Belgium NV*, not yet reported, para. 89.

35 Ibid., para. 89.

36 Ibid., paras. 90 to 95.

37 Ibid., paras. 96 to 115.

law, the Court itself obviously denied a third ground for justification in *Ålands Vindkraft*[38] and *Essent Belgium*[39] by expressly referring to Article 36 TFEU and overriding requirements only. A reconstruction of the justification concept that applies to the principle of free movement of goods can theoretically be based on three different approaches. First, Article 36 TFEU, which allows for the justification of discriminatory measures, is to be interpreted in such a way as to ensure it covers those national measures which are aimed at environmental protection although this objective is not mentioned in Article 36 TFEU. However, this requires a wide interpretation of an exemption rule which does not follow the logic of rule (which is free movement of goods) and exemption (Article 36 TFEU).[40]

Second, the *Cassis* formula now fully applies to discriminatory measures. For this approach, it should be recalled that the Court in *Ålands Vindkraft* and in *Essent Belgium* mentioned overriding requirements as a ground for justification – a wording which is known from the original *Cassis* formula. Furthermore, environmental protection – expressly assessed by the Court in both judgments – is regarded as a mandatory requirement within the meaning of *Cassis*. It should, however, be considered that the Court has developed a non-exhaustive list of mandatory requirements not all of them being of the same value as the internal market with its principle of free movement of goods. Mandatory requirements are any reasons within the umbrella concept of public interests with the exception of purely economic reasons.[41] Therefore public interests such as fiscal supervision and the fairness of commercial transactions, for example, are regarded as mandatory requirements and may justify trade restrictions. Not all mandatory requirements of that non-exhaustive list are objectives of the EU with the same value as the principle of free movement of goods. Considering this, it seems to be necessary to avoid an inflationary use of the *Cassis* exemption by establishing two sets of categories of mandatory requirements:[42] the first category comprising of those mandatory requirements which are of the same value as the principle of free

38 C-573/12 *Ålands Vindkraft*, not yet reported, para. 76.

39 Joint cases C-204/12 to 208/12, *Essent Belgium NV*, not yet reported, para. 89.

40 Craig and de Burca take a different view: *Craig/de Burca*, EU Law, (OUP, 5th ed. 2011), p. 678.

41 *Chalmers/Davies/Monti*, European Union Law (Cambridge University Press, 2010), p. 766.

42 Fontanelli takes a different view: *Fontanelli*, The Essent judgment: Another revolution in the case law on free movement of goods? Online: http://eulawanalysis.blogspot.co.uk/2014/09/the-essent-judgment-another-revolution.html (last access: 11.11.2014).

movement of goods, the second one comprising of all other mandatory requirements which are not of the same value as the principle of free movement of goods.

The first category, for example, comprises of environmental protection, consumer protection and fundamental rights – all of them of the same value as the principle of free movement of goods. The list of those objectives is exhaustive as it only contains those interests which the Treaties attach the same importance to as to the free movement of goods. Article 3 and 6 TEU, Article 11 and 12 TFEU provide for an important role of environmental protection, fundamental rights and consumer protection. If a national measure aims to attain one of these objectives, it can be justified even if its nature is discriminatory. The second category of mandatory requirements covers those public interests which are not of the same value as free movement of goods and can only justify trade restrictions that are caused by national measures which apply equally to domestic and to imported products. The list of those interests is non-exhaustive; their use is limited.

The concept of justification, reconstructed in the way formerly described, ensures the free movement of goods as one of the cardinal principles of European integration on the one hand, and fully ensures the attainment of other important objectives of European integration (by national measures), on the other. It is furthermore in line with the approaches of the Court in the aforementioned judgments.

VI. Conclusion

The ongoing dialogue between the principle of free movement of goods, which limits the freedom of the national legislative bodies, and the national renewable energy promotion schemes, which have challenged traditional limitations to the free movement of goods three times, has required rethinking and reconceptualising the concept of justifications to restrictions on trade within the meaning of Article 34 TFEU. It now seems to be settled case-law that national discriminatory measures attaining to an objective of equal value to the principle of free movement of goods can be justified, even if that objective is not mentioned in Article 36 TFEU. The list of those objectives is exhaustive, whereas the list of mandatory requirements which are not of the same value as free movement of goods is non-exhaustive. The justification on the grounds of these second-class mandatory requirements under the *Cassis* formula is still limited to non-discriminatory measures. This approach adequately ensures the fulfilment of all objectives the European Union attaches importance to.

Sirja-Leena Penttinen
PhD Researcher, Lecturer, UEF Law School
University of Eastern Finland
sirja-leena.penttinen@uef.fi

The *Essent* Case – the one about free movement, economic justifications and the increasing role of the State

Content

I. Introduction

On 22 October 2013 the Grand Chamber of the Court of Justice of the European Union (hereinafter 'the Court') gave its judgment in case C-105–107/12 *Essent and Others*. This case adds an interesting new chapter to the saga of the development of one of the fundamental freedoms – the free movement of capital – and (once again) to the relationship between the energy sector and publicly owned companies. In particular, the judgment sheds light on the Court's current approach to Article 345 TFEU and the system of property ownership as well as on restrictions on capital movement and their possible justification. The multiple elements present in the case mean that it has further implications both for the energy sector and more generally in relation to capital movement, thus shaping this field of law and thereby also impacting on economic and monetary union. In addition, it should be noted that Article 63 TFEU departs from the other free movement provisions as it also protects capital movement with third countries. Therefore the third country aspect of free movement of capital especially regarding ownership unbundling should not be overlooked.

II. Background

The subject-matter of the proceedings was Dutch national legislation implementing the second set of electricity and gas directives.[1] This legislation laid down three set of rules governing (1) the prohibition of privatisation; (2) group prohibition; and (3) the prohibition of 'unrelated activities'.

The rules governing the prohibition of privatisation require that shareholders belonging to the 'circle of authorities' must both own the shares in the distribution system operator companies and have control of the systems. This 'circle' consists of public authorities, such as municipalities, provinces or the State or legal entities wholly owned, whether directly or indirectly, by the same. Only these authorities may be or may become shareholders in a system operator. Following from this, authorisation for any alteration in the ownership of a system or shareholding in a system operation must be refused if it is likely to result in the shares passing into the ownership of persons outside the circle of authorities. As a consequence, only

---

1 Directive 2003/54/EC of the European Parliament and of the Council of 26 June 2003 concerning common rules for the internal market in electricity and repealing Directive 96/92/EC (OJ L 176, 15.7.2003, pp. 37–55); and Directive 2003/55/EC of the European Parliament and of the Council of 26 June 2003 concerning common rules for the internal market in natural gas and repealing Directive 98/30/EC (OJ L 176, 15.7.2003, pp. 57–78).

public authorities may own the distribution system operators, whether directly or indirectly, and private investors are excluded.

The provisions governing the group prohibition are to the effect that system operators cannot be members of a group or even otherwise connected with a group to which any energy company producing, supplying or marketing electricity or gas in the Netherlands also belongs. Thus, in order to comply with this prohibition, vertically integrated energy undertakings must be broken up in order to create one or more system operators responsible for the operation of the system on the one hand; and energy companies responsible for the production, supply and trade of electricity or gas on the other.

The prohibition of unrelated activities comprises three elements. First, a distribution system operator and group companies connected with it may not engage in transactions or other activities which may conflict with the interests of a system operation. This prohibition also prevents a group company from carrying on activities not closely linked with basic infrastructure tasks. Lastly, the prohibition prevents the system operator from supplying financial guarantees or standing as a guarantor of debts incurred by other divisions of the distribution system operator.

According to the Netherlands Government, when the national legislation entered into force three types of undertakings were active on the Dutch energy market: (1) undertakings active only in electricity or gas production, supply or trade; (2) vertically integrated undertakings active both in electricity or gas production, supply or trade and in the operation and use of electricity and gas distribution systems; and (3) undertakings principally active in the operation and use of electricity and gas systems that did not engage in activity relating to electricity or gas production, supply or trade.

The applicant undertakings, *Essent NV*, *Essent Nederland BV*, *Eneco Holding* and *Delta NV*, were the major vertically integrated energy companies acting on the Dutch market and thus belonged to the second category of undertakings.

Under the applicable national legislation, these companies had to be wholly owned, either directly or indirectly, by public shareholders belonging to the circle of authorities. In turn, the members of the circle of authorities were prohibited from selling the system or the system operator, or any parts of these, to private investors. *Essent NV* has since split into two companies: *Enexis Holding NV* is a system operator, which, in accordance with the prohibition of privatisation, is wholly owned by public shareholders; and *Essent NV* is responsible for the marketing, supply and production of electricity and gas. The two other companies have remained vertically integrated companies but have identified their subsidiaries as being the operators of their distribution systems.

These companies brought three separate actions before the national courts claiming that the group prohibitions and the prohibition of unrelated activities run counter to the fundamental freedoms of freedom of establishment and free movement of capital provided for in Articles 49 and 63 TFEU and are therefore of no effect. The Netherlands' defence was that the prohibition of privatisation constitutes a body of rules governing the system of property ownership within the meaning of Article 345 TFEU. It followed from this (ran the argument) that shares held in a system operator cannot be the subject of private investment and that either the Treaty provisions on free movement of capital and freedom of establishment are inapplicable or, alternatively, that such prohibition is justified on the grounds of overriding reasons in the public interest. The Supreme Court of the Netherlands (Hoge Raad der Nederlanden) referred three identically worded questions to the Court for a preliminary ruling.

First of all, the national court enquired whether the wording in Article 345 TFEU that 'the rules in Member States governing the system of property ownership' should be taken to cover rules relating to the absolute prohibition of privatisation under which shares in a system operator can be transferred only within the circle of public authorities. If so, the referring court wished to know whether this meant that the rules relating to the free movement of capital do not apply or are not even taken into account in respect of the group prohibition and the prohibition of unrelated activities. The third question related to objectives behind the provisions. The national court asked whether the objectives of achieving transparency in the energy market and preventing distortion of competition by opposing cross-subsidisation (which also inform the Dutch national legislation) amount to purely economic interests, or whether they can also be regarded as interests of a non-economic nature, in the sense that in certain circumstances they may constitute justification for restriction of the free movement of capital.

1. Opinion of the Advocate General

AG Jääskinen delivered his Opinion on 16 April 2013.[2] He stated that the prohibition of privatisation constitutes a body of rules governing the system of property ownership which falls under the scope of Article 345 TFEU. As such, it is compatible with EU law. In relation to the second and third questions, he reached, in essence, a similar conclusion as the Court, but adopted a slightly different line of argumentation. Interestingly, AG Jääskinen raised the question of whether the

2 AG Jääskinen in C-105/12–107/12 *Essent and Others*, not yet reported.

unbundling of ownership structures provided for in the Third Energy Package[3] is compatible with the provisions of the Treaty and in particular with the free movement provisions which ownership unbundling is likely to restrict. Ownership unbundling has been a rather hotly debated topic but property rights have provided the main focus of such debate.[4] The emphasis, however, is not on the fundamental rights aspect as such but instead on the fundamental freedoms. Therefore although the Court did not address this issue in detail in its judgment but simply Stated that the grounds for overriding reasons in the public interest were in accordance with the objectives pursued by the Third Energy Package Directives, it is worth briefly considering the AG's reasoning on it. As the AG noted in his conclusions, the problem may present itself elsewhere later on and further guidance might then be welcome.

By examining the possible justification of the prohibition of privatisation on the ground of overriding reasons in the public interest, AG Jääskinen emphasised the special characteristics of electricity and gas distribution systems and the importance of opening these network-bound sectors to fair competition. Furthermore, he examined the effect of secondary EU law in relation to the transposition of the provisions of the 2003 electricity and gas directives into national law. He held that the 2003 directives do not require the unbundling of ownership of shares in a transmission or distribution system operator and ownership of shares in other traders. Therefore, it seems that the Dutch legislation went further than was required by the directives, which, as AG Jääskinen stressed, provide only for a minimum level of harmonisation.

However, he held that even though the electricity and gas directives of the Third Energy Package are not applicable to the present case, their subsequent adoption cannot be disregarded since, unlike their predecessors, they make ownership

---

3 Electricity Market Directive and Gas Market Directive.

4 See, e.g., the following contributions: *Talus/Hunt*, Ownership Unbundling: What End to the Saga? in: Buschle/ Hirsbrunner/Kaddous (eds.), European Energy Law, Droit européen de l'énergie (Bruylant, 2011), pp. 25–50; *Pielow/Brunekreeft/Ehlers*, Legal and economic aspects of ownership unbundling in the EU, 2 (2) Journal of World Energy Law and Business (2009), pp. 96–116; *Talus/Johnston*, Comment on Pielow, Brunekreeft and Ehlers on "ownership unbundling", 2 (2) Journal of World Energy Law & Business (2009), pp. 150–151; *del Guayo/Kühne/Roggenkamp*, Ownership Unbundling and Property Rights in the EU Energy Sector in: McHarg/Barton/Bradbook/Godden (eds.), Property and the Law in Energy and Natural Resources (OUP, 2010), pp. 326–357; *Hunt*, Ownership Unbundling: The Main legal Issues in a Controversial Debate in: Delvaux/ Hunt/Talus, EU Energy and Policy Issues, ELRF Collection, 1st ed. (Euroconfidentiel 2008), pp. 33–90.

unbundling a specific method of transposition. While the recitals to the directives appear only to relate to transmission systems, AG Jääskinen, the Government of the Netherlands and the European Commission all regarded them as relevant to distribution systems due to the special characteristics of such systems and the need to eliminate conflicts of interests between system operators and users. AG Jääskinen viewed the elimination of conflicts of interest as being an equally pressing goal in respect of distribution systems as it is for transmission systems, even though only the latter is decisive when it comes to the freedom to provide services on a cross-border basis.

As AG Jääskinen pointed out, given the current State of EU energy law, the group prohibition and the prohibition of unrelated activities cannot be challenged without reviewing the compatibility of the 2009 directives with the principle of free movement of capital. He noted, however, that the ownership unbundling provided for in the directives is not as far-reaching as the group prohibition since the possibility for reciprocal minority investments between a system operator and a production or supply undertaking remains open. Following from this, he raised the question of whether the ownership unbundling provided for in the 2009 Directives is compatible with the provisions on free movement which the ownership unbundling is likely to restrict.

AG Jääskinen referred to the settled case-law on the matter, which indicates that the EU legislature is bound by the principle of freedom of movement in the same way as national legislatures. In the case of *Bauhuis*[5] the Court explicitly stated that measures enacted by the Council in the general interests of the EU and not unilaterally by the Member States in order to protect their own interests cannot be regarded as measures impeding trade. As a presumption, secondary EU legislation is, at least in principle, in conformity with the free movement provisions. AG Jääskinen also referred to *Germany v Parliament and Council*[6] in which the Court held that the objective of combating any market disturbance could justify a restriction on freedom of establishment stemming from secondary legislation. Such an objective could not, however, be used to justify a similar national measure that was purely economic in nature.

As a result, AG Jääskinen concluded that the economic aims of the Treaty may justify restriction on fundamental freedoms stemming from EU legislation. He also noted that this problem may present itself in the same terms outside the realm of the liberalisation of the electricity and gas distribution system sectors. This

---

5 C-46/76 *Bauhuis* [1977] ECR 5, paras. 27–30.

6 C-233/94 *Germany v Parliament and Council* [1997] ECR I-2405, para. 57.

may prove to be the case especially in relation to national competition legislation which may prove to be stricter than that of the EU and thus likely to constitute a restriction on freedom of establishment.

2. Judgment of the Court

The Court started by looking at the first two questions together: i.e. whether the Dutch prohibition of privatisation falls under the scope of Article 345 TFEU, and if so, whether it then follows from this that Article 63 TFEU does not apply to national measures prohibiting ownership or control links between certain group companies.

The Court stated that 'Article 345 TFEU is an expression of the principle of the neutrality of the Treaties in relation to the rules in Member States governing the system of property ownership'.[7] In previous cases its stance has been that the Treaties do not, as a general rule, preclude either the nationalisation or privatisation of undertakings.[8] Therefore, Member States may, in principle, legitimately establish or maintain national provisions regulating public ownership of certain undertakings.

The prohibition of privatisation provided for in the Dutch legislation permits shares held in a distribution system operator to be transferred only to the authorities or to legal entities owned, either directly or indirectly, by the authorities. It follows that the prohibition prevents any private individual from owning shares in an electricity or gas distribution system operator active in the Netherlands. The objective of the national measure is therefore to maintain a body of rules relating to public ownership that affects operators. Such a prohibition should be regarded as falling within the scope of Article 345 TFEU.

However, the prohibition of privatisation also has other implications. It prevents undertakings established in other Member States and active in electricity or gas production, supply or trade, as well as companies located in other Member states that are members of the same group as such an undertaking, from acquiring shares in an electricity or gas distribution system operation active in the Netherlands. This amounts to a group prohibition, and as such is obviously not compatible with the Treaty provisions on the free movement of capital as it clearly

---

7 C-105/12–107/12 *Essent and Others*, not yet reported, para. 29.

8 6/64 *Costa v Enel* [1964] ECR 585 and C-244/11 *Commission v Greece*, judgment given on 8 November 2012, not yet reported.

prevents the main methods by which capital may be transferred.[9] The Court very straightforwardly Stated that the fact that Article 345 TFEU expresses the principle of neutrality of the Treaties regarding the Member States' system of property ownership does not mean that rules governing the system of property ownership currently in force in the Member States are not subject to the fundamental rules of the TFEU. It went on to say that even though the Netherlands had established a body of rules relating to public ownership within the scope of Article 345 TFEU in the energy sector, this did not mean that Member States are free to disregard the rules relating to the free movement of capital. Consequently, the prohibition of privatisation, together with the group prohibition and prohibition of unrelated activities, fall within the scope of Article 63 TFEU and must therefore be examined in the light of that article.

The Court held that national measures must be regarded as impediments in the light of Article 63(1) TFEU if they are liable to prevent or limit the acquisition of shares in the undertakings concerned or deter investors from other Member States from investing in their capital. In addition, as the Court has previously held,[10] national measures imposing quantitative or qualitative restrictions on investments made in other Member States has a restrictive effect on undertakings established in other Member States. As a consequence, restrictive provisions enacted at national level constitute obstacles to the raising of capital, inter alia, by restricting the acquisition of shares. Following from the prohibition of privatisation, private investors cannot acquire shares or other forms of interest in the capital of an electricity or gas distribution system operator active in the Netherlands.

In addition, an undertaking from another Member State that is a member of the same group as an undertaking active in the production, supply or trade of electricity or gas in the Netherlands may not acquire shares in a company that is a member of the same group as a system operator active in the Netherlands. Furthermore, a company belonging to the same group as a system operator in the Netherlands may not invest in an undertaking established in another Member State that is active in the production, supply or trade of electricity or gas in the

---

9 The Court expressly noted that the TFEU does not define the notion of the concept of movement of capital within the meaning of Article 63(1) TFEU. It had previously recognised as having indicative value the nomenclature of capital movements set out in Annex I to Council Directive 88/361/EEC of 24 June 1988 for the implementation of Article 67 of the [EC] Treaty (OJ L 178, 8.7.1988, pp. 5–18). On the basis of the Directive, the Court has held that capital movements include, in particular, so-called direct investments and portfolio investments.

10 C-271/09 *Commission v Poland*, judgment given on 21 December 2011, not yet reported.

Netherlands. The same applies in respect of companies that are members of the same group as such an undertaking. In addition to the group prohibition, the prohibition of unrelated activities may also entail qualitative restrictions on investments in other Member States. These are aimed at preventing, either directly or indirectly, companies in the same group as a distribution system operator active in the Netherlands from investing in undertakings active in sectors other than system operation. All of the above-mentioned prohibitions contained in the national legislation constitute restrictions on the free movement of capital within the meaning of Article 63 TFEU, even though Article 345 TFEU covers the public ownership system established in the Netherlands.

The third question referred for a preliminary ruling was whether the objectives behind the national legislation – combating cross-subsidisation, achieving transparency in the electricity and gas markets and preventing distortions of competition – amount to purely economic interests or whether they could be considered to fall within the ambit of overriding reasons in the public interest and thus justify restrictions on trade.

As is commonly known, restrictions on capital flows may be justified either on the grounds listed in Article 65 TFEU or on the basis of overriding reasons in the public interest established in the Court's legal praxis. The Court reiterated the view that it has repeatedly expressed in the past that grounds of a purely economic nature cannot constitute overriding reasons in the public interest. Nevertheless, it has accepted in previous cases that controversial national legislation may be justifiable if prompted by economic reasons that serve an objective in the public interest.[11] On this occasion, the Court Stated that although the prohibition of privatisation falls within the scope of Article 345 TFEU, which cannot justify restrictions on to the free movement of capital, this does not mean that the interests behind the national legislative measures relating to the distribution system operator's ownership issues may not be taken into account as an overriding reason in the public interest.

Following this line of argumentation, the Court referred to two of its earlier judgments in which it had stated that Article 345 TFEU cannot justify restrictions on trade, but emphasised that these judgments were comparable with the scenario at hand.[12] The earlier judgments related to restrictions created by certain

11 C-141/07 *Commission v Germany* [2008] ECR I-6935, para. 60; C-158/96 *Kohll* [1998] ECR I-1931, para. 50, C-444/05 *Stamatelaki* [2007] ECR I-3185, para. 31.

12 C-274/06 *Commission v Spain* [2008] ECR I-26 and C-271/09 *Commission v Poland*, judgment of 21 December 2011, not yet reported.

privileges or restrictions that ultimately had no effect on the rules relating to ownership issues.

By contrast, in the case at hand the national measures involved imposed an absolute prohibition on privatisation. On this basis, the Court held that the reasons behind adopting national legislation in respect of the ownership of the property, which falls within the scope of Article 345 TFEU, constitute factors which may be taken into account as circumstances capable of justifying restrictions on the free movement of capital, but that it was up to the national court to make this assessment.

The Court approached the group prohibition and the prohibition of unrelated activities by examining whether, by reference to their objectives, the national measures involved were instituted on the basis of overriding reasons in the public interest. The Court referred to the preamble of the TFEU, which States that in order to achieve, inter alia, fair competition for the protection of consumers – a legitimate key interest recognised by the Court – there is a need for concerted action. Similarly, the objective of guaranteeing adequate investment in electricity and gas distribution systems is primarily designed to ensure the security of the energy supply – a legitimate key interest recognized by the Court – as well as one of the triple objectives of the common European energy policy.

The Court also referred to the objectives underlying the electricity and gas directives, which were to establish an open and transparent market, facilitate non-discriminatory and transparent access to the network of the distribution system operator and to create a level playing field. While the Court made reference to the 2003 directives, the importance of achieving such objectives has only increased over time – as noted by AG Jääskinen, the same objectives inform the Third Energy Package. The Court took the view that even if the group prohibition and the prohibition of activities which may adversely affect system operation were not imposed by the directives, the Netherlands nevertheless pursued, by adopting controversial measures, the objectives sought by the 2003 directives. In conclusion, the Court held that '[...] the objectives referred to by the referring court may, in principle, as overriding reasons in the public interest, justify the identified restrictions on fundamental freedoms'.[13] However, it was left for the referring national court to determine whether the national measures pass the traditional proportionality test.

13 C-105/12–107/12 *Essent and Others*, not yet reported, para. 66.

III. Comments

1. The Court's approach to Article 345 TFEU and the system of property ownership

The Court's judgment is important for several reasons. Firstly, it provides guidance on the Court's current approach to Article 345 TFEU governing Member States' systems of property ownership. Secondly, it questions the traditional approach to justifying trade restrictions where the objectives sought can be considered to be purely economic. Thirdly, looking at the bigger picture, it raises interesting questions in relation to the increasing role of the State in the EU energy market and the application of free movement law.

The lineage of Article 345 can be traced back to the Schuman Declaration of 1950.[14] Despite such longevity, the precise application and meaning of the Article remains somewhat unclear due to its very broad wording. It stipulates that the Treaties shall not prejudice the system of property ownership in the Member States which, at first glance, would seem to indicate that they will not in any way affect the systems of property ownership of the Member States. In fact, the Article should be interpreted in a more neutral way: the EU has a neutral attitude when it comes to the Member States' systems of property ownership and how they are regulated.[15] It is, however, unsurprising that the Article features in an energy-law-related case: the energy sector is largely characterised by State intervention and ownership unbundling has been the subject of lively debate since the 1990s.[16]

---

14 The very first provision concerning property issues was included in Article 83 of the Treaty establishing the European Coal and Steel Community in 1951. An almost identical provision of what is today known as Article 345 was included in Article 222 of the Treaty establishing the European Economic Community in 1957, which later became Article 295 of the Treaty establishing the European Community. For more on the development of Article 345 TFEU, see *Losada/Juutilainen/Havu/Vesala*, Property and Integration: Dimensions of Article 345 TFEU, 3 Juridiska Föreningen i Finland (2012), pp. 203–209.

15 For a more detailed analysis of Article 345 TFEU, see *Akkermans/Ramaekers*, Article 345 TFEU, Its Meanings and Interpretations, 3 (16) European Public Law (2010), pp. 292–314.

16 Following from the results received by the energy sector inquiry (the DG Competition report on energy sector inquiry (SEC(2006)1724, 10 January 2007)), the Commission considered that the opening up of the EU wide energy markets was linked to the further unbundling of energy networks. Resulting from this, further unbundling of vertically integrated companies exercising both network operations, such as transport and/or distribution, and commercial activities, such as generation and/or supply, was proposed.

It should, however, be noted that Article 345 governs the rules on the *system* of property ownership, not the rules of property ownership itself. Therefore, the Treaties do not affect the choice of the system of property ownership – this remains within the competence of the Member States. However, the Article does not confer absolute immunity from the application of Treaty rules to property rights. This is due to the fact that a certain degree of unification is needed in order to achieve economic integration.[17] EU internal market law focuses on ensuring the free movement of goods, services, persons and capital and has wide application due to the process of economic integration. The application of internal market law to areas involving property law is therefore natural even though property law issues are usually considered to be within Member States' national competences.[18] Consequently, keeping in mind the economic aims of EU integration, it is no surprise that the Court held that rules governing the system of property ownership are subject to the fundamental rules of the TFEU, including those concerning the prohibition of discrimination, freedom of establishment and the free movement of capital.[19] As a result, Member States remain free to choose the way in which they organise their ownership structures but must keep within the limits set by the Treaty provisions concerning free movement.

2. Purely economic aims as a justification for trade restrictions

The grounds on which barriers restricting EU-wide trade may be justified fall into two categories: grounds for justification provided in the Treaty and the so-called mandatory requirements developed by the Court in its case-law. Both of these justification categories are based on the idea of ensuring that the criteria of overriding public interest are met. If a legitimate public interest can be identified, the national measure must still be in conformity with the general principles of EU

Provisions on ownership unbundling were later introduced in the Third Energy Package Directives. For an overview of the regulatory evolution in respect of unbundling see *Talus/Hunt*, Ownership Unbundling: What End to the Saga? in: Buschle/Hirsbrunner/Kaddous (eds.), European Energy Law, Droit européen de l'énergie (Bruylant, 2011), pp. 25–50.

17 *Talus/Johnston*, Comment on Pielow/Brunekreeft/Ehlers on "ownership unbundling", 2 (2) Journal of World Energy Law & Business (2009), pp. 150–151.

18 *Akkermans/Ramaekers*, Free Movement of Goods and Property Law, Maastricht European Private Law Institute, Working Paper No. 2011/26, p. 1.

19 Similarly, C-452/01 *Margarethe Ospelt* [2003] ECR I-9743 and C-309/96 *Annibaldi* [1997] ECR I-7505.

law, the principle of proportionality in particular.[20] However, the Court has often refused to accept any grounds for the justification of national measures that aim to achieve objectives of an economic nature. The same applies both to Treaty-based justifications and to mandatory requirements.[21] Nevertheless, even though the Court has generally condemned economic aims, it has in practice allowed them in certain circumstances, either by interpreting the concept of restriction narrowly to avoid the issue of justification altogether, by linking the economic aims to other public interest considerations or by denying or ignoring the economic nature of the objectives sought.[22]

The third question referred for a preliminary ruling dealt with the objectives of an economic nature, as the national Court asked the Court whether the elements involved in combating cross-subsidisation, including the exchange of strategic information, in order to achieve transparency in the electricity and gas markets, and to prevent distortions of competition, constitute purely economic interests; or whether, on the contrary, they are overriding reasons in the public interest capable of justifying restrictions on the free movement of capital. In answering the questions the Court reiterated, by referring to settled case-law, that grounds of a purely economic nature cannot constitute overriding reasons in the public interest justifying restrictions of free movement provisions.[23] However, as mentioned above and noted by the Court in the present case, the Court has accepted that national measures – even if the measures would be of

---

20 See, e.g., 204/12–08/12 *Essent Belgium*, not yet reported, para. 89. It should, however, be noted that certain legitimate key interests recognised by the Court, such as environmental protection, were first recognised by the Court as mandatory requirements but later also included under Treaty-based grounds for justification. As such they were included within the scope of the protection of the health and life of humans, animals or plants, thus extending the scope of the Article. See, e.g., 204/12–08/12 *Essent Belgium*, not yet reported, para. 93. Therefore, it can be argued that there is a degree of overlap between the two categories and it is not always clear under which heading a certain public interest objective falls. It is, however, important to determine which category to choose, as the requirements for the application of Treaty-based grounds for justification differ from the mandatory requirements.

21 See, e.g., 288/83 *Commission v Ireland* [1958] ECR 1761, C-164/99 *Portugaia Construções* [2002] ECR I-787, C-324/93 *Evans Medical* [1995] ECR I-563.

22 *Snell*, Economic Aims as Justification for Restrictions on Free Movement' in: Schrauwen (ed.), Rule of Reason: Rethinking another Classic of EC Legal Doctrine (Europa Law Publishing, 2005).

23 C-105/12–107/12 *Essent and Others*, not yet reported, para. 51.

an economic nature – may constitute a justified restriction on a fundamental freedom if they pursue an objective in the public interest.

In the case at hand, the Court held that the reasons underlying the choice of rules of property ownership adopted in the national legislation constitute factors which may be taken into consideration as circumstances capable of justifying restrictions on the free movement of capital. This, according to the Court, is to be left to the referring court to assess.

However, in respect of the other prohibitions, the Court took a rather surprising step in the reasoning it adopted in respect of the objectives of an economic and non-economic nature. It stated that guaranteeing adequate investment in a distribution system is designed to ensure security of supply – an overriding reason in the public interest. More interestingly, the Court held that the objective of achieving undistorted competition is also an objective pursued by the Treaty. In this connection it referred to fair competition, which has the ultimate aim of protecting consumers. This reasoning skates on thin ice because, according to the Court, consumer protection constitutes an overriding reason in the public interest and therefore measures to avoid undistorted competition also constitute overriding reasons in the public interest.[24]

It is clear from this line of reasoning that fitting economic aims into the notion of overriding public interest poses serious challenges for the Court. In doing this, it tends to link economic aims to other, more commonly known, public interest considerations.

However, in this particular case the economic aims sought by adopting the contested national measures do not seem to have been adopted solely in order to achieve protectionist objectives, which is the main reason why economic aims are not in general accepted as grounds for justification. As the Court itself noted, the

24 AG Jääskinen was neither convinced by the linkage between consumer protection and public security on one hand, nor by group prohibition and the prohibition of unrelated activities on the other. His view was that neither the adequacy of those measures nor their proportionality to those objectives was clear. He took the view that the prohibition of privatisation was already sufficient to meet the requirements arising from the need to ensure public security, since such prohibition excludes, inter alia, the operation of electricity distribution systems by companies controlled by third States. Opinion of Advocate General Jääskinen in C-105/12–107/12 *Essent and Others*, not yet reported, para. 88. On the other hand, it has also been presented that the possible social benefits that could derive from ownership unbundling for consumers would be regarded as being in the general interest, for more on this issue, see *Hunt*, Ownership Unbundling: The Main legal Issues in a Controversial Debate in Delvaux/Hunt/Talus, EU Energy and Policy Issues, ELRF Collection, 1st ed. (Euroconfidentiel 2008), p. 87.

group prohibition and the prohibition of unrelated activities were introduced by national legislation implementing the 2003 electricity and gas directives into the Dutch legal system. These directives sought, inter alia, to establish an open and transparent market, non-discriminatory and transparent access to the network of the distribution system operator and a level playing field. These objectives were even more clearly highlighted in the 2009 directives, although these were not yet in force at the time the Dutch legislation was adopted. However, as the national legislation went further than required by the directives, AG Jääskinen took the view that national measures should therefore be detached from the 'pure' transposition measures of the 2003 directives and reviewed the measures in the light of the principle of free movement of capital.

Despite the fact that the Third Energy Package Directives were not applicable at the given time, the Court placed emphasis on the objectives pursued by these regulatory measures. This was done even though a literal and restrictive interpretation of the 2009 electricity and gas directives seems to suggest that they only concern transmission system operators.[25]

However, the same objectives are also relevant to distribution system operators even if only the transmission systems are decisive from the point of view of freedom to provide services on a cross-border basis.[26] It can therefore be argued that the public interest objectives present in the case are not only purely one particular Member State's protectionist measures – even though they went further than required by the directives[27] – but instead reflect the overall objectives of integration of the EU energy market. Consequently, the objectives and their protection should be seen through the EU lens instead of assessing the nature of

---

25 Only operational and legal unbundling of the distribution system operators both for electricity and gas was required by the Directives: '[w]here the distribution system operator is part of a vertically integrated undertaking, it shall be independent at least in terms of its legal form, organization and decision making from other activities not relating to distribution. Those rules shall not create an obligation to separate the ownership of assets of the distribution system operator from the vertically integrated undertaking.' Article 26(1) of the Electricity Market Directive and Article 26(1) of the Gas Market Directive.

26 Opinion of AG Jääskinen in C-105/12–107/12 *Essent and Others*, not yet reported, paras. 70–72. This view was also shared by the Dutch Government and the Commission.

27 For more detailed analysis on the minimum and maximum harmonisation, see *Weatherill*, Maximum versus Minimum Harmonisation: Choosing between Unity and Diversity in the Search for the Soul of the Internal Market in: Shuibhne/Gormley (eds.), From Single Market to Economic Union, Essays in Memory of John A Usher, (OUP, 2012), pp. 175–199.

the objectives purely from the viewpoint of one single Member State. This was also noted by AG Jääskinen, who suggested a 'new approach to economic grounds', on the basis of which he sought to distinguish between economic grounds that protect, in one way or another, the economic interests of the Member States, and economic grounds that organise a sector in accordance with the economic aims of the Treaty, thus emphasising the overall public interest of the whole of the EU.[28]

The objectives pursued also distinguish the case at hand from the so-called *Golden Shares* cases.[29] In the *Golden Shares* cases restrictions on capital movements were imposed by national measures that bestowed privileges on public authorities by granting them shareholdings in privatised companies with certain special rights.

In these cases, national measures focused on safeguarding Member States' national protectionist interests; while in the case at hand State holdings in distribution system operators were intended to enhance competitiveness in both the electricity and the gas markets in Netherlands.

Consequently, it follows from the judgment that it could be argued that purely economic reasons still cannot justify trade restrictions – or at least the Court has not said as much out loud – if the objective does not also serve a wider public good at EU level. Thus, the Court still does not find Member States' protectionist measures to be justifiable per se. That said, a measure that does go further than is necessary and required by the directive, but still reflects the same objectives and values[30] – even if economic in nature – as lie behind the EU-wide legislation can be accepted. This is an aspect of the wider discussion on the balancing of economic integration against welfare protection that takes place within the EU.[31]

---

28 Opinion of AG Jääskinen in C-105/12–107/12 *Essent and Others*, not yet reported, para. 95. A similar view was expressed in the earlier Opinion of AG Saggio in C-127/97 *Burstein* [1998] ECR I-6005, para. 24. Here, the focus was on the circumstances under which Member States may adopt stricter national measures than provided for in the secondary legislation. AG Saggio held that '[t]he difference in the procedure, and the greater power accorded to Member States as a result, is justified by the consideration that any more stringent measures adopted by the Member State are *aligned with*, rather than constituting a derogation from, *the objective of the relevant [EU] provision*'. (emphasis added).

29 See, e.g., C-438/99 *Commission v France* [2002] ECR I-4781& C-367/98 *Commission v Portugal* [2002] ECR I-4731.

30 Or '[...] certain standards believed to be reasonable across the [EU] [...]' as described by *Unberath/Johnston*, The Double-Headed Approach of the CJEU Concerning Consumer Protection, 5 (44) CMLRev (2007), p. 1240.

31 For more on this issue, see *Maletić*, The Law and Policy of Harmonisation in Europe's Internal Market (Edward Elgar, 2013).

The Court opined that the objectives in question amounted to overriding reasons in the public interest and as such could in principle justify the restrictions on fundamental freedoms. Nevertheless, the general rule is that such measures need to be proportionate. Assessment of this issue was left to the referring court to determine. It would naturally be interesting to see how the national court weighs the principle of proportionality against the restrictive measures.

3. The increasing role of the State and free movement law in the EU energy sector

The role of States in relation to the energy sector has been at issue since energy was first brought up in discussions on market integration. It was clear from the beginning that energy differs from all other economic sectors due to its vital importance to society in general.[32] It was therefore held to belong strictly to the domain of State sovereignty. Thus, energy markets have been characterised by the presence either by State monopolies or of national companies with special privileges and close ties to the government controlling the markets.[33] As a result very little action was taken in relation to the energy sector at EU level prior to the 1980s.

However, the impetus provided by the general single market programme also increased the focus on energy step by step. National energy companies were no longer able to rely on the public service obligation provisions (now contained in Article 106 TFEU) and could therefore be exempted from the application of free movement provisions or the general provisions of competition law. In the 1990s the Commission brought two sets of infringement proceedings before the Court claiming that the exclusive rights enjoyed by national champions were contrary to Treaty provisions on the free movement of goods and freedom of establishment and could not be justified on the grounds of public service obligations under what is now Article 106(2) TFEU.[34]

---

32 Also noted by the Court in C-72/83 *Campus Oil* [1984] ECR 2727, para. 34.

33 For a comprehensive overview, see *Talus*, EU Energy Law and Policy: A Critical Account (OUP, 2013), pp. 269–286.

34 C-157/94 *Commission v Netherlands* [1997] ECR I-5699, C-159/94 *Commission v Italy* [1997] ECR I-5793; C-158/94 *Commission v France* [1997] ECR I-5819. For more on this issue, see *Penttinen*, The Role of the Court of Justice of the European Union in the Energy Market Liberalization in: Talus (ed.), Research Handbook on International Energy Law (Edward Elgar, 2014), pp. 251–253.

These were the first free movement related energy cases after *Campus Oil*[35] and *Commission v Greece*,[36] which concerned the issue of security of supply. The liberalisation process followed this, relying on secondary legislation. Since then, the process of opening up the markets has relied more on competition law provisions.

The First Energy Package at the end of the 1990s only introduced the idea of opening up the EU-wide energy market. However, the Second Energy Package of 2003 accelerated the move towards a more market-based approach with the help of competition law and the hype surrounding the concept of a market-driven energy sector continued. However, it rather soon became clear that an approach based solely on the market could not fully deliver what was needed. Accordingly, from as early as the Third Energy Package a gradual move began from a purely market-based mechanism towards a mixed regime in which the role of the State and public sector actors is increasingly significant.[37] This can be seen in many areas. It is especially clear in respect of energy (infrastructure) investments – the case at hand, in which the involvement of private investors is excluded, provides just one example of this – as well as in the (desired) increase in renewable energy production.[38]As a result, despite the market-driven approach, the role of the State has been gradually increasing.

While the functioning of the energy markets in the context of the market-driven approach has relied almost entirely on the competition law provisions, the rules of free movement law have had little impact. This follows naturally from choices made in the past: due to the sector's special nature which is marked by national interests, it was easier to seek to accomplish the opening of the market on the basis of competition law provisions than on the basis of those on free movement, since the former did not interfere directly with issues of State sovereignty whereas the scope of the free movement law always encompasses Member States and their actions.

Recently, the Court has received references for preliminary rulings in which the emphasis has been on internal market law rather than competition law, as in the case at hand.[39] These cases have raised the question of whether the secondary law provisions conform with the primary law on free movement.

---

35 C-72/83 *Campus Oil* [1984] ECR 2727.

36 C-347/88 *Commission v Greece* [1990] ECR I-4747.

37 See also European Commission Press Release, 13 November 2008, MEMO/08/743.

38 *Talus*, European Union Energy: New Role for States and Markets in: Belyi/Talus (eds.), States and Markets in Hydrocarbon Sectors (Palgrave, 2015).

39 See, e.g., C-573/12 *Ålands Vindkraft*, not yet reported; C-204 to C-208/12 *Essent Belgium*, not yet reported.

This in turn raises the following questions: (1) whether regulation of the market under secondary law has, at least in part, been the result of a rather weak integration process; and (2) whether the regulation can, in fact, keep up with the pace at which events are unfolding on the energy market. The speed at which such developments are taking place is influenced by several factors drawn from both inside and outside the EU's borders. These include the shale gas boom and the results of the policies adopted, such as the push for renewable energy production – both of which require State intervention – but also include many other factors from outside the energy sector that have implications on the field. The ongoing Ukrainian crisis is just one example of this.

However, the increasing need for State control has caused cases to be brought before the Court that relate, surprisingly, to free movement law. Given the current State of the EU energy law it might be reasonable to argue that questions relating to free movement law will increasingly come to the fore together with questions on the relationships between different market players. The increasing role of the State does not, however, mean a return to the old pre-liberalisation state of play but instead presents a sort of halfway house situation. This could lead to the re-emergence of free movement law in the energy sector.

IV. Conclusion

The judgment handed down in the case of Essent and Others contains many enlightening features. It contributes to the ongoing discussion of the role of States in today's EU energy markets by revising the limits of State intervention in energy companies. When the case is placed in the context of current developments as described above, the end result does not appear as that much of a surprise. In addition, the debate on the limits of the competences of Member States and the EU has been ongoing for many decades.

This is reflected especially in the justification of trade barriers in intra-EU trade, where national regulatory autonomy is respected up to a certain point, in particular regarding positive harmonisation, by setting 'only' minimum harmonisation requirements, as was the case with regard to the 2003 directives. If, however, Member States propose more stringent measures in the positive harmonisation context the Court often seeks to increase the effectiveness of the perceived objective by means of secondary legislation.

From this viewpoint, it is little wonder that the Court decided to accept the interests in question, which were of an economic nature but were also reflected at EU level, as overriding reasons in the public interest capable of justifying restrictions on the free movement of capital. Reaching the opposite decision would clearly have hindered the realisation of the objectives behind the Third Energy Package Directives, which were already in force at the time the judgment was delivered. In this light, the Court also seems to have established a level playing field on which Member States are able to contribute to the realisation of the internal market through national property law choices. This seems to follow naturally from the current phase of development of the EU energy sector where the role of the State is gradually becoming more supervisory in nature.

From a more practical point of view, the judgment has significance especially for private investors. By stating that Member States are free to determine whether certain activities in the energy sector may be undertaken only by public undertakings, in accordance with Article 345 TFEU, the Court excluded the possibility of private investors acquiring shares or interest in the capital of a distribution system operator active in the Netherlands. From this perspective, it will be interesting to see whether this has further and wider implications in other Member States.

Kim Talus
Professor of European Energy Law at UEF Law School (University of Eastern Finland) and a Professor of Energy Law at University of Helsinki
kim.talus@uef.fi

Renewable Energy Disputes in the European Union: An Overview of Current Cases

Content

I. Introduction[1]

Energy disputes come in many shapes and forms and involve many different areas of law. On the public international law side, boundary and territorial disputes are common.[2] Where new areas with hydrocarbon potential are discovered, interest in the exact location of a maritime border is suddenly heightened, as was the case in the recent Eastern Mediterranean when the Leviathan field was discovered.[3] Energy and natural resources are also a major focus of investment disputes in the field of public international law. This is illustrated by the ICSID[4] statistics, which show that around 30% of all investment disputes under the ICSID framework relate to energy.[5] In fact, many of the key arbitral awards that have shaped the details of investment treaty arbitration come from the energy sector, with internationalisation of contracts and damage calculations being among the areas particularly impacted by energy disputes.[6] At European Union (EU) level, several energy cases have come before the Court of Justice of the European Union (CJEU).[7] Here too, disputes take various forms. Cases come before the General Court as a result of disputed elements of the European Commission's administrative practice in such areas as the application of EU competition law.[8] The CJEU decides cases referred

1 Kim Talus is a Professor of European Energy Law at UEF Law School (University of Eastern Finland) and a Professor of Energy Law at University of Helsinki. He is also the Editor-in-Chief for OGEL (www.ogel.org) and an expert member (electricity) at the Finnish Market Court. He can be contacted at kim.talus@uef.fi. The present article represents some preliminary views and research on the subject matter. An OGEL special issue will be published on this issue in early 2015.

2 For an overview of the issues, see *Martin*, Energy and International Boundaries Resolution in: Talus (ed.), Research Handbook on International Energy Law (Edward Elgar, 2014).

3 See the OGEL special issues on Eastern Mediterranean (3/2013).

4 International Centre for Settlement of Investment Disputes.

5 The ICSID Caseload – Statistics (Issue 2013–1), ICSID, 2, available at https://icsid.worldbank.org/ICSID/FrontServlet?requestType=ICSIDDocRH&actionVal=CaseLoadStatistics (last accessed on 13 August 2014).

6 For discussion, see *Sabater/Stadnyk*, International Arbitration and Energy: How Energy Disputes Shaped International Investment Dispute Resolution in: Talus (ed.), Research Handbook on International Energy Law (Edward Elgar, 2014).

7 For an overview, see *Penttinen*, The role of the Court of Justice of the European Union in the energy market liberalization in: Talus (ed.), Research Handbook on International Energy Law (Edward Elgar, 2014). See also *Talus*, EU Energy Law and Policy: A Critical Account (OUP, 2013).

8 T-360/09 *E.ON Ruhrgas and E.ON v Commission*, judgment of 29 June 2012.

to it for a preliminary ruling under Article 234 of the TFEU[9] or as the final stage of infringement proceedings.[10]

These cases involve an element of EU law which has had an impact on the operations of a private party. National proceedings ascend to EU level when the national court applies for a preliminary ruling on the interpretation of a particular point of EU law. While many of the earlier energy related cases heard by the CJEU related to the free movement provisions contained in EU treaties,[11] more recent cases have often focused on questions of third party access to energy networks and the interpretation of the sector-specific regulatory framework,[12] although a change is this respect has been seen over the last few years with several free movement cases coming before the CJEU.[13] Moving to the contract law side, there are frequent contractual disputes in the energy sector. These arise as a result of the long-term nature of the energy business, the unpredictable circumstances impacting energy contracts and the economic balance sought through contractual arrangements. The gas price disputes in the EU are a good illustration of this.[14] Similarly, many disputes that took place during the liberalisation of power markets in the Nordic countries show the impact of change of circumstances on

9 Cases like C-393/92 *Almelo v NV Energiebedrijf Ijsselmij* [1994] ECR I-1477; C-17/03 *VEMW and others* [2005] ECR I-4983; C-206/06 *Essent Netwerk Noord and Others* [2008] ECR I-05497; C-439/06 *Citiworks AG Flughafen Leipzig v. Halle GmbH, Bundesnetzagentur*, [2008] ECR I-3913 or C-265/08 *Federutility and others* [2010] ECR I-03377.

10 Cases like 347/88 *Commission v Greece* [1990] ECR I 4747; C-157/94 *Commission v Netherlands* [1997] ECR I-5699; C-158/94 *Commission v Italy* [1997] ECR I-5789; C-159/94 *Commission v France* [1997] ECR I-5815; C-160/94 *Commission v Spain* [1997] ECR I-5851; C-213/96 *Outokumpu* [1998] ECR I-1777; C-379/98 *PreussenElektra*, [2001] ECR 2099.

11 Cases like 72/83, *Campus Oil v Minister for Industry* [1984] ECR 2727 (Ireland); 347/88 *Commission v Greece* [1990] ECR I 4747; C-157/94 *Commission v Netherlands* [1997] ECR I-5699; C-158/94 *Commission v Italy* [1997] ECR I-5789; C-159/94 *Commission v France* [1997] ECR I-5815; C-160/94 *Commission v Spain* [1997] ECR I-5851; C-379/98 *PreussenElektra*, [2001] ECR 2099.

12 C-17/03 *VEMW and others* [2005] ECR I-4983; C-206/06 *Essent Netwerk Noord and Others* [2008] ECR I-05497; C-439/06 *Citiworks AG Flughafen Leipzig v. Halle GmbH, Bundesnetzagentur*, [2008] ECR I-3913; C-239/07 *Julius Sabatauskas and Others*, [2008] ECR I-7523, or C-264/09 *Commission v Slovak Republic* [2011] ECR I-08065.

13 See the contribution of *Penttinen* in this publication.

14 These have been discussed in detail in *Hober*, Recent Trends in Energy Disputes in: Talus (ed.), Research Handbook on International Energy Law (Edward Elgar, 2014).

pre-existing contractual arrangements.[15] To a limited extent, the nature of the disputes has to do with the energy carrier or energy form. Disputes relating to oil and gas often differ somewhat from, say, those relating to nuclear energy.

Oil and gas deposits are both extremely valuable and very much fixed to a location. Nuclear power has certain inherent risks and externalities and all operations are under strict governmental control, with focus on security. Having said this, while such differences exist, it would be a step too far to suggest that energy disputes can be categorised by reference to the form of energy involved. Nuclear disputes can relate to the construction, as do those in other areas of energy like renewable, LNG or oil. As correctly noted by Kaj Hober:

[I]t is not possible to identify any recent trend common to energy disputes in general. Those trends which are discernible seem to be specific to the nature of the energy dispute in question. The only identifiable common denominator is – not surprisingly – that energy disputes reflect the general financial, political and geopolitical developments in the world economy.'[16]

This article focuses on renewable energy disputes in the EU. It does not confine itself exclusively to disputes relating to EU law, but instead covers different types of renewable energy related disputes that have recently arisen in the EU area. These may involve issues of public international law, EU law, private law and contractual arrangements. The article examines these three types of disputes and analyses their backgrounds and the reasons why they arose. Recent and ongoing renewable energy disputes under international law have concerned international investment law and WTO law. However, recent renewable energy disputes at European level have mostly related to the free movement provisions of EU Treaty law. Contractual arrangements and connection issues serve as illustrations of private and contractual disputes in these areas.

II. Renewable energy in the European Union

The EU and its Member States have recently pushed for a greener energy mix involving a significantly increased share for renewable energy. Nuclear energy,

---

15 These have been discussed in *Rajala/Kärkkäinen*, Pitkien tukkusähkösopimusten vaikutukset sähkön vähittäismyynnin kilpailutilanteeseen (Effects of long-term wholesale contracts on the competitive situation in electricity sales). Report commissioned by Ministry of Trade and Industry on 3 August 1998. Studies and Reports 7/1999. Available in Finnish only.

16 *Hober*, Recent Trends in Energy Disputes in: Talus (ed.), Research Handbook on International Energy Law (Edward Elgar, 2014).

the other viable option to reduce CO^2 emissions, has received much less EU-level attention. This is no doubt due to the less controversial and less politically charged nature of renewable energy production.

EU measures to promote renewable energy have ranged from requiring that Member States provide priority access to the electricity networks in respect of electricity produced from renewable sources to setting mandatory targets for the share of renewable energy for all Member States.[17] Without going so far as to create an EU-level scheme to support renewable energy production, the EU has allowed and encouraged Member States to set up support mechanisms for electricity generation from renewable sources. It has been left to individual Member States to decide on the content of these support mechanisms.

The backbone for the EU measures in this area is provided by the 20–20–20 by 2020 objectives set in 2007.[18] For renewable energy, these objectives aim at a 20% overall share of renewable energy production in the EU by 2020. Currently, the European Commission's proposal is that this EU-level objective should be increased to 30% by 2030. The 20–20–20 by 2020 objectives also include energy efficiency and CO^2 emissions targets which are, however, beyond the scope of the present article. Likewise, since this article focuses on renewable electricity production and related disputes, biofuel objectives are not covered here.[19] The overall objective of a 20% share for renewable energy in the EU is translated into national objectives. Unlike the situation under the previous legal regime,[20] the RES Directive made these objectives binding on States.

The binding nature of the renewables targets has meant a considerable increase in investment in this method of producing electricity in the EU. However, this trend is not limited to Europe, as investment in this area has increased globally.

---

17 For details, see *Penttinen/Talus*, The development of Sustainability Aspects in EU Energy Law, Research Handbook in Climate Change Mitigation Law (Edward Elgar, 2015).

18 European Commission, Renewable Energy Road Map Renewable energies in the 21st century: building a more sustainable future (COM(2006) 848 final), Brussels, 10.1.2007.

19 These have been discussed in *Penttinen/Talus*, The development of Sustainability Aspects in EU Energy Law, Research Handbook in Climate Change Mitigation Law (Edward Elgar, 2015). See also *Johnston/Block*, EU Energy Law (OUP, 2012).

20 Directive 2001/77/EC of the European Parliament and of the Council of 27 September 2001 on the promotion of electricity produced from renewable energy sources in the internal electricity market, (OJ L 283, 27.10.2001, pp. 33–40).

Renewable energy production is nothing new: windmills have been used to produce wind-based energy and dams have been used to produce mechanical energy for centuries past. However, the scale of investment in this area and the increased regulation of and drive towards this type of electricity generation is unprecedented. Given the surge in activity in renewable energy production, it is no surprise that disputes in this area have started to arise.

Issues that have led to disputes within the EU and globally have, for example, related to the national governments' objective of ensuring maximum national or regional benefit from governmental measures in this area (similar to what is done in oil and gas-producing countries through local content requirements), miscalculations of subsidies in the planning stages and excessive costs for the State from such subsidies, especially when economic circumstances have changed.

Furthermore, the scale of activities has in itself contributed to all kinds of disputes arising. The following sections examine and discuss renewable energy disputes under public international law (section III), EU law (section IV) and private and contractual law (section V). The last section concludes the article.

III. Energy disputes in the sphere of public international law

As noted in the introduction, a significant number of global investment disputes relate to the energy and resources sectors. Those arising in the energy sector do not only concern developing countries or, for example, Latin American countries, since in recent years EU Member States have also been involved in such disputes. The Energy Charter Treaty (ECT), originally an instrument for EU-Russia investment and supply of energy products, has alone provided the applicable rules of international law for 58 disputes, many of which have been intra-EU disputes.[21] These disputes have often related to the ongoing process of energy market liberalisation initiated in the 1980s. Fundamental changes in the regulatory environment and approach to energy markets, from State to markets, has created risks for investors and investments. Similarly, recent cases have related to changes in energy policy, as in the German nuclear case.[22] Some of the most recent EU cases in this area of international law have come from the renewable energy sector, and many were initiated in the context of the ECT.

Given the need for subsidies and other forms of State support for renewable energy projects, investment in this area is heavily dependent on the public sector,

---

21 For the list of publicly known cases, see http://www.encharter.org.

22 *Vattenfall vs. Germany* (ICSID Case No. ARB/12/12).

host States' energy policies and regulatory frameworks, and changes in these. Investors cannot expect regulations or even policies to remain unchanged. Regulatory frameworks change. States have the right to changes their energy policies. While investors must predict and adapt to such changes, they are subject to certain boundaries. In the EU context, the CJEU has noted that legitimate expectations and the principle of legal certainty do not mean that an individual or investor can expect legislation to remain unchanged, but only that the special circumstances of the economic actors involved would be taken into account when amending the legislation.[23]

In another case, the CJEU reaffirmed that 'the principle of legal certainty requires, particularly, that rules of law be clear, precise and predictable in their effects, in particular where they may have negative consequences on individuals and undertakings.'[24]

In terms of international law in respect of energy, the role of the ECT is to lay down the conditions and limits for State intervention in the renewable energy sector. Enforced through international arbitral tribunals, the checks and boundaries in place offer a degree of investment certainty in this area.

The fact that government subsidies provide the backbone for renewable energy investment makes such investment particularly vulnerable to changes in law and policy. The record number of claims relating to investment brought against Spain illustrates the consequences for renewable energy of changes in the regulatory framework and to rules relating to subsidies. The feed-in-tariff (FIT) for electricity produced from renewable source (and co-generation) in Spain was established in order to attract investment in this sector of the energy market. The original scheme applied to all electricity produced from renewable sources during the lifetime of the projects and entitled the generator to a FIT. Due to the change in economic circumstances and lack of State financial resources, combined with the fact that the scheme was perhaps too generous in the first place, Spain made two modifications to it, with retrospective applicability to all projects. First, in 2010 the State limited the period during which renewable projects could benefit from the FIT scheme. Since this involved significant economic consequences for investment in this area, this change led, unsurprisingly, to litigation at the Supreme Court of Spain. The ensuing judgment noted that the changes made in 2010 should be

23 C-17/03 *VEMW and others* [2005] ECR I-4983.

24 Case C-347/06 *ASM Brescia SpA v Comune di Rodengo Saiano* [2008] ECR I-5641.

considered as mere adjustments to the existing scheme and were reasonable in terms of the economic objective they were based on.[25]

Then in July 2013, the Spanish government approved Royal Decree-Law 9/2013 which completely abolished the tariff regulation and replaced it with a new remuneration scheme. The new calculations for remuneration were not based on energy produced but on installed capacity and the exploitation costs of a standard facility.[26] In addition, the 2013 changes included a 7% tax increase for power generation, which due to the different treatment of renewables and fossil-fuel-based power production, impacted and targeted only renewable energy production (these producers had no ability to pass on the costs to the final consumer).

The tax carve-out contained in Article 21 of the ECT could be one of the reasons why the government took this approach. These events have led to numerous cases against Spain. So far, 11 cases relating to Spain and the changes described above have been initiated before investment tribunals, and 2014 alone saw 6 new cases initiated before ICSID tribunals.[27]

While the Spanish cases are perhaps the most well-known, other claims have been brought against many other EU Member States on similar grounds: cases

---

25 JUR 2014/14099.

26 This regime has been described in many commercial online publications, such as http://www.cliffordchance.com/briefings/2013/07/royal_decree-law92013of12julyonth.html.

27 For example, *PV Investors v. Spain* (Registered in November 2011 under the ad hoc UNCITRAL Arbitration Rules); Charanne (the Netherlands); *Construction Investments (Luxembourg) v. Spain* (Registered in 2013 under Arbitration Institute of the SCC); *Isolux Infrastructure Netherlands B.V. v. Spain* (2013, Arbitration Institute of the SCC); *CSP Equity Investment S.à.r.l. v. Spain* (June 2013, Arbitration Institute of the SCC); RREEF; *Infrastructure (G.P.) Limited and RREEF Pan-European Infrastructure Two Lux S.à.r.l. v. Spain* (November 2013, ICSID Case No. ARB/13/30); *Antin Infrastructure Services Luxembourg S.à.r.l. and Antin Energia Termosolar B.V. v. Spain* (November 2013, ICSID Case No. ARB/13/31); *Eiser Infrastructure Limited and Energia Solar Luxembourg S.a.r.l. v. Spain* (December 2013, ICSID Case No. ARB/13/36); *Masdar Solar & Wind Cooperatief UA v. Spain* (February 2014, ICSID Case No. ABR/14/01); *NextEra Energy Global Holdings B.V. and NextEra Energy Spain Holdings B.V. v. Spain* (May 2014, ICSID Case No. ABR/14/11); *InfraRed Environmental Infrastructure GP Ltd. et al v. Spain* (June 2014, ICSID Case No. ABR/14/12); *RENERGY S.à.r.l. v. Spain* (2014, ICSID Case No. ABR/14/18).

involving the Czech Republic,[28] Italy[29] and Bulgaria[30] are examples of these. It also seems that new cases will be initiated against States like Romania or Germany.[31] In addition to investment disputes, national renewable energy schemes have also been the subject of proceedings at WTO level. *Dispute DS412, Canada — Certain Measures Affecting the Renewable Energy Generation Sector*, which involved Canadian domestic content requirements, offers an example of this.

The requirements in question had to be met by certain generators of electricity that utilised solar photovoltaic and wind power technology in relation to the design and construction of electricity generation facilities in order for these generators to qualify for guaranteed prices offered under the FIT Programme. This programme was adopted by the Government of the Province of Ontario, as well as by all individual FIT and micro-FIT Contracts implementing these requirements since the FIT Programme's inception in 2009.

For example, the Ontario Green Energy and Economy Act accepts solar projects only if at least 40% of their initial development comprises Ontario products and services.

In this case, Japan claimed that the domestic content requirements included in the Canadian measures constituted a violation of: (i) the national treatment obligation under Article III:4 of GATT 1994; (ii) the prohibition set out in Article 2.1 of the TRIMs Agreement on the application of any trade-related investment measures that are inconsistent with Article III of GATT 1994; and (iii) the prohibition on import substitution subsidies prescribed in Articles 3.1(b) and 3.2 of the SCM Agreement. Eventually both the WTO panel and the Appellate Body found that the Canadian local content obligation conflicted with the national

---

28 *Voltaic Network GmbH v. Czech Republic* (May 2013, UNCITRAL ad hoc); *ICW Europe Investments Limited v. Czech Republic* (May 2013, UNCITRAL ad hoc); *Photovoltaik Knopf Betriebs-GmbH v. Czech Republic* (May 2013, UNCITRAL ad hoc); *WA Investments-Europa Nova Limited v. Czech Republic* (May 2013, UNCITRAL ad hoc); *Mr. Jürgen Wirtgen, Mr. Stefan Wirtgen, and JSW Solar (zwei) v. Czech Republic* (June 2013, UNCITRAL ad hoc) *Antaris Solar and Dr. Michael Göde v. Czech Republic* (May 2013, UNCITRAL, PCA administered); *Natland Investment Group NV, Natland Group Limited, G.I.H.G. Limited, and Radiance Energy Holding S.A.R.L. v. Czech Republic* (May 2013, UNCITRAL ad hoc).

29 *Blusun SA, Jean-Pierre Lecorcier and Nichael Stein v. Italy* (February 2014, ICSID Case No. ABR/14/03).

30 *EVN AG v. Republic of Bulgaria,* ICSID Case No. ARB/13/17.

31 This suggestion is based on the discussions at the 'Arbitration of Energy Disputes' conference in Copenhagen (1–2 September 2014) where the author chaired the renewable energy session.

treatment obligation and violated GATT Article III:4 as well as Article 2.1 of the TRIMs Agreement.[32]

As noted by many scholars, the report did not deal with the FIT or the pre-renewable energy policies but instead only found a violation with respect to the discriminatory nature of the local content requirement.[33] On 5 June 2014, Canada informed the WTO system that the Government of Ontario had complied with the recommendations and rulings by: (i) no longer subjecting large renewable electricity procurements to domestic requirements; and (ii) significantly lowering the domestic content requirements for small and micro-FIT procurement of wind and solar electricity under the FIT Programme.

In another case relating to renewable energy, *Dispute DS452, European Union and Certain Member States — Certain Measures Affecting the Renewable Energy Generation Sector,* China raised somewhat similar questions vis-à-vis the EU FIT scheme, including domestic content restrictions, that affect the renewable energy generation sector relating to EU Member States' feed-in tariff programmes, including but not limited to Italy and Greece. China claims that these measures are inconsistent with Articles I, III:1, III:4 and III:5 of GATT 1994; Articles 3.1(b) and 3.2 of the SCM Agreement; and Articles 2.1 and 2.2 of the TRIMs Agreement. No progress has yet been reported in respect of this case.

Another local content-related, but not directly EU-related, case is that of *China – Measures concerning Wind Power Equipment.*[34] The facts of this case are that Chinese policy included a local-content requirement for wind energy projects, which increased to 70% in 2010 when China's domestic wind industry had been fully established. This policy encouraged international players to set up manufacturing facilities in China. Consultations initiated by the US were quickly ended and

---

32 *Kulovesi,* International Trade Disputes on Renewable Energy: Testing Ground for the Mutual Supportiveness of WTO Law and Climate Change Law, 23:3 Review of European Community and International Environmental Law (2014).

33 *Kulovesi,* 'International Trade Disputes on Renewable Energy: Testing Ground for the Mutual Supportiveness of WTO Law and Climate Change Law', 23:3 Review of European Community and International Environmental Law (2014). See also *Leal-Arcas/Filis,* Certain Legal Aspects of the Multilateral Trade System and the Promotion of Renewable Energy, Queen Mary University of London, School of Law, Legal Studies Research Paper No. 166/2014; or *Leal-Arcas,* Unilateral Trade-related Climate Change Measures, The Journal of World Investment & Trade 13 (2012), pp. 875–927.

34 WTO: *China – Measures concerning Wind Power Equipment,* Request for consultations by the United States, WT/DS419/1, 6 January 2011.

China agreed to withdraw the disputed subsidies forthwith.[35] These are just a few examples of proceedings at WTO level. Many more are pending.[36] These cases relate to various aspects of renewable energy production and the applicable regulatory framework. Since they are currently pending, little information on progress is available.

IV. Renewable energy disputes in the sphere of European Union law

Renewable energy disputes have also arisen in the context of EU law. One of the first cases on this topic, the *Outokumpu*[37] case, came from Finland. It related to discriminatory national treatment through environmental taxation and concerned excise duty on electricity imported into Finland from Sweden. The well-known case of *PreussenElektra*[38], in turn, concerned a feed-in-tariff scheme in which electricity supply companies were obliged to purchase electricity generated from renewable sources in their areas at a fixed price considerably higher than the price of electricity produced from non-renewable sources. This purchase obligation only covered renewable energy generated in Germany and was *de facto* discriminatory. The scheme raised two separate issues, which were addressed by the CJEU: (i) that of State aid for environmental purposes and the requirement that aid is granted by a Member State or through State resources; and (ii) the relationship between the TFEU's free movement of goods provisions and environmental protection. As to the second question addressed by the CJEU, the outcome of the case was favourable to the national scheme, despite its clearly discriminatory nature.

After considering various issues relating to the facts of the case, including the generally positive impact of renewable energy production on the environment and the implementation of the United Nations Framework Convention on Climate Change and its Kyoto Protocol, the need to protect the health and life of humans,

---

35 'China Ends Wind Power Equipment Subsidies Challenged by the United States in WTO Dispute', Office of the United States Trade Representative Press Release, June 2011, found at: <http://www.ustr.gov/about-us/press-office/press-releases/2011/june/china-ends-wind-power-equipment-subsidies-challenged>.

36 For an overview, see *Leal-Arcas/Filis*, Certain Legal Aspects of the Multilateral Trade System and the Promotion of Renewable Energy, Queen Mary University of London, School of Law Legal Studies Research Paper No. 166/2014; or *Leal-Arcas*, Unilateral Trade-related Climate Change Measures, The Journal of World Investment & Trade 13 (2012), pp. 875–927.

37 Case C-213/96 *Outokumpu* [1998] ECR I-1777.

38 Case C-379/98 *PreussenElektra*, [2001] ECR 2099.

animals and plants, the integration principle under Article 11 of the EU Treaty, the priority given to the production of electricity from renewable sources, the ongoing process of liberalisation and the difficulties involved in determining the origins of energy once it has been introduced into the electricity grids, the CJEU found that '[h]aving regard to all the above considerations, the answer to the third question must be that, in the current State of Community law concerning the electricity market, legislation such as the amended *Stromeinspeisungsgesetz* is not incompatible with Article 30 of the Treaty [now Article 36 TFEU].'

Given the increased focus on environmental considerations within the EU today, as enshrined in Article 11 of the EU Treaty, it is not surprising that the case-law of the CJEU clearly holds that national measures capable of obstructing intra-EU trade may be justified by overriding requirements relating to the protection of the environment, provided that the measures in question are proportionate to the aim pursued.[39] The latest additions to the CJEU's case-law relating to renewable energy are the cases C-573/12, *Ålands Vindkraft AB v. Energimyndigheten*; and C-204/12–C-208/12, *Essent Belgium NV v Vlaamse Reguleringsinstantie voor de Elektriciteits- en Gasmarkt.* The issues at stake in these two cases are not insignificant: they involve the entire construction of the EU's efforts to increase the amount of electricity produced from renewable energy sources and curb CO^2 emissions from electricity generation.

The decision in C-573/12, *Ålands Vindkraft AB v. Energimyndigheten* was handed down on 1 July 2014. Essentially, the CJEU followed its earlier case-law, including *PreussenElektra*, and allowed the Member States to establish support schemes for renewable energy, restricted to energy produced within that Member State:

> '1. Point (k) of the second paragraph of Article 2 and Article 3(3) of Directive 2009/28/EC of the European Parliament and of the Council of 23 April 2009 on the promotion of the use of energy from renewable sources and amending and subsequently repealing Directives 2001/77/EC and 2003/30/EC must be interpreted as allowing a Member State to establish a support scheme, such as that at issue in the main proceedings, which provides for the award of tradable certificates to producers of green electricity solely in respect of green electricity produced in the territory of that State and which places suppliers and certain electricity users under an obligation to deliver annually to the competent authority a certain number of those certificates, corresponding to a proportion of the total volume of electricity that they have supplied or consumed.

39 Case C-320/03, *Commission v. Republic of Austria* [2005] ECR, I-9871, para. 70; Case C-463/01, *Commission v. Germany* [2004] ECR, I-11705, para. 75; Case C-309/02, *Radlberger Getränkegesellschaft and S. Spitz* [2004] ECR, I-11763.

> 2. Article 34 TFEU must be interpreted as not precluding national legislation, such as that at issue in the main proceedings, which provides for the award of tradable certificates to green electricity producers solely in respect of green electricity produced in the territory of the Member State concerned and which places suppliers and certain electricity users under an obligation to surrender annually to the competent authority a certain number of those certificates, corresponding to a proportion of the total volume of electricity that they have supplied or used, failing which they must pay a specific fee.
>
> 3. It is for the national court to determine, taking into account all relevant factors — which may include the EU legislative context in which the legislation at issue in the main proceedings arises — whether, in terms of its territorial scope, that legislation meets the requirements of the principle of legal certainty.'

Prior to the judgment, the Advocate General came to a very different conclusion and suggested that the existing EU renewables scheme, which is based on national systems, should be abolished as it is contrary to the EU free movement rules.

While the CJEU's judgment is in many ways the right one, and thus expected,[40] the argumentation employed in it is not very convincing. That provided by the Advocate General appears more robust. There is little doubt that the CJEU's approach has much to do with political realities and the need to support measures that help curb CO^2 emissions, as the sections from the judgment reproduced below illustrate.

Section 90 of the judgment States as follows:

> 'In the second place, it must be Stated that, given the fungible nature of the electricity in the transmission and distribution systems, those guarantees (guarantees of origin) cannot serve as confirmation that a certain volume of electricity supplied by those networks is precisely the electricity from renewable energy sources in respect of which those guarantees were given and, accordingly, the systematic identification of electricity as green electricity at the distribution and consumption stages remains difficult to put into practice.'

Section 99 of the judgment states:

> 'Furthermore, as was also noted by the EU legislature in recital 25 to Directive 2009/28, it is essential, in order to ensure the proper functioning of the national support schemes, that Member States be able to "control the effect and costs of their national support schemes according to their different potentials," while maintaining investor confidence.'

Neither of these arguments (and these are just examples) are very convincing. The same points were addressed by the Advocate General, with a very different outcome. The CJEU, no doubt recognising political realities around renewable

40 *Talus*, EU Energy Law and Policy: A Critical Account (OUP, 2013).

energy and climate change, does not really address the core issues of free movement and environmental issues.

Instead it follows the approach taken in its earlier *PreussenElektra* judgment – one nicely characterised by Henrik Bjørnebye as a 'smorgasbord of arguments and considerations'.[41]

The other recent case, *Essent Belgium*,[42] was decided on 11 September 2014. The CJEU, as was very much expected given its judgment in the *Ålands Vindkraft*, concluded that Member States may provide incentives for electricity suppliers to support the production of green electricity by domestic producers. It held that the limitation placed on the free movement of goods caused by this can be justified on the basis of environmental considerations; and more specifically, on the basis of the public interest involved in promoting the use of renewable energy sources. Looking at these two recent judgments, at the earlier cases of *PreussenElektra*[43] and *Bluhme*,[44] and at the efforts made at international, EU, and national level to reduce greenhouse gas emissions and curb climate change, it might not be excessively rash to suggest that, where necessary in order to provide an effective response to the looming environmental crises, the CJEU is prepared to adopt a more relaxed approach to measures taken by Member States than it would in other situations.[45]

In essence, it is prepared to accept that the application of law must be sensitive to the surrounding realities. As such, it does not lightly strike down effective and proportionate environmental measures taken at national level.[46] Given the rationale of these judgments and the continuing relevance of Article 11 TFEU, now coupled with the increasing urgency of the need to reduce greenhouse gas emissions, it would seem that measures introduced or specifically allowed through secondary EU law would comply (*de facto* at the very minimum[47]) with TFEU

41 *Bjørnebye*, Investing in EU Energy Security: Exploring the Regulatory Approach to Tomorrow's Electricity Production (Kluwer Law International, 2010), p. 108.

42 C-204/12–C-208/12 *Essent Belgium NV*, not yet published.

43 C-379/98 *PreussenElektra*, [2001] ECR 2099.

44 C–67/97 *Bluhme* [1998] *ECR* I–8033.

45 *Chalmers/Davies/Monti*, European Union Law (Cambridge University Press, 2010), p. 896.

46 *Talus*, EU Energy Law and Policy: A Critical Account (OUP, 2013).

47 Compare this to the solution under general EU competition law (Articles 101 and 102 TFEU) where the approach has sometimes been to circumvent the difficult questions of quantifiability or the non-economic nature of the benefit by not dealing with these issues. See *K. Talus*, Vertical natural gas transportation capacity, upstream commodity contracts and EU competition law (Kluwer Law International 2011). For the role of environmental gains under the public procurement rules, see Case C-513/99 *Concordia Bus Finland* [2002] ECR I-7213.

rules on the free movement of goods, even where these have a discriminatory effect.[48]

While Energy Community is a separate international organization, it is very much an instrument of EU external energy relations and as such, is worth mentioning under the section for EU disputes. Energy Community Treaty was signed on 25 October 2005 by the European Union and the (now nine) Member States of the Energy Community.

The substantive provisions of the Energy Community Treaty mirror some of the Articles of the TFEU and in addition the framework identifies certain EU law instruments which the Member States have to implement. Among these is the RES Directive. On 2 October 2014 the Energy Community Secretariat opened a Preliminary Procedure against one of its Member States, Ukraine,[49] for possible violations of the RES Directive and Article 7 of the Energy Community Treaty, which prohibits discrimination. Much like the WTO case involving local content, the case against Ukraine relates to a local content clause in the Electricity Law of Ukraine. Under this clause, eligibility for feed-in tariffs for investments in renewable energy depends on the fulfilment of minimum shares of goods and works of Ukrainian origin (local content). With direct references to the Canadian case, the Energy Community Secretariat has challenged the Ukrainian scheme.

V. Renewable energy disputes in the sphere of contract law

Much like the examples discussed above, increased commercial and investment activity in the renewable energy sphere has naturally led to an increase in litigation and disputes in relationships between private parties. Disputes over connection to the grid have in particular arisen in the context of renewable energy projects, especially in the context of offshore projects where connection to the onshore grid is not cheap. One example of this is the delays in grid connections in Germany.[50]

---

48 However, Johnston et al. suggest that Article 11 TFEU only refers to the EU legislator and would not help where the question relates to compatibility with Treaty provisions. See *Johnston et al.*, The Proposed New EU Renewables Directive: Interpretation, Problems and Prospects, 1(3) European Energy and Environmental Law Review (2008), p. 134.

49 Case ECS-7/13. See http://www.energy-community.org/portal/page/portal/ENC_HOME/NEWS/News_Details?p_new_id=9581.

50 http://www.windpowermonthly.com/article/1124483/players-dispute-cable-delay-claims.

Commercial disputes have also arisen in relation to product quality.[51] The struggle between the parties in the Greater Gabbard Offshore Wind Farm project is one example of this. Here the disputes related to claims and counterclaims on 'standard of build relating to 52 upper and 35 lower foundations at the 140-turbine array' and 'compensation for schedule and cost impacts arising from delays, disruption and productivity issues'.[52]

Other areas of disputes include questions of default, take-or-pay contracts, price variations and so on.[53] These disputes mostly involve elements of normal contract interpretation and are not really new or specific to renewable energy or even to energy in general.

VI. (Preliminary) analysis and conclusions

Disputes covered in this article derive from various areas of law: public international law, EU law, and private law and contractual disputes. While it is difficult to map specific reasons or trends for these disputes, they do seem to have two factors in common. Most of the cases relate to government regulation (or changes in regulation) and/or the scale of activities in this area of energy. The underlying issue in these cases is not new: it is that of investor rights versus the right of States to regulate. The answer lies in fair treatment for investors: protection of legitimate expectations and the economic balance of the original deal.

Renewable energy investment relies heavily on public subsidies and the surrounding regulatory framework. Changes in these areas during the lifetime of the project will significantly affect the business case for the investment. Where changes take place, investors react. Investment arbitration involving Spain and other EU countries followed changes in the regulatory frameworks that had been relied on by the investor. States restrict foreign participation in the energy sector and in the renewable energy sector for various reasons. Local content requirements are common in the oil and gas industry.

Similarly, requirements of national content have been applied to the renewable energy sector. Requirements relating to the need to establish a local company

---

51 http://www.thecourier.co.uk/business/news/great-gabbard-offshore-wind-turbine-dispute-settled-1.93694.

52 http://www.thecourier.co.uk/business/news/great-gabbard-offshore-wind-turbine-dispute-settled-1.93694.

53 This suggestion is based on the discussions at the 'Arbitration of Energy Disputes' conference in Copenhagen (1–2 September 2014) where the author chaired the renewable energy session.

to participate in the oil and gas industry are common. Again, similar requirements have been established for the renewable energy sector. The EU case of *Ålands Vindkraft* and under the WTO dispute settlement mechanism case *Dispute DS412, Canada — Certain Measures Affecting the Renewable Energy Generation Sector* both relate to restrictions on foreign participation. In Sweden, the law required that the project must be located in the territory of Sweden. In the Canadian scheme, the law required that a portion of the equipment had to be manufactured in Canada. Mirroring the WTO disputes, the recent Energy Community proceedings raise similar issues. One common element in the EU and WTO cases relating to renewable energy is decision-making bodies' reluctance to address the main issue at stake and thus undermine national efforts to curb emissions: the main issue being the compatibility of renewable energy schemes with WTO or EU law. On this point, Kati Kulovesi has noted that 'the reluctance of the panel and Appellate Body to classify the FIT scheme as a subsidy in the *Canada - Renewable Energy* case can arguably be understood by reference to tensions underlying the relationship between renewable energy support measures and WTO law.'[54]

A somewhat similar comment could be made in relation to the CJEU's two most recent renewable energy judgments: *Essent* and *Ålands Vindkraft*. The possible incompatibility of a FIT with the applicable legal rules is either not addressed, as in the WTO case; or is dismissed on the strength of unconvincing argumentation, as in the EU cases. Thus the urgency of the need to put in place measures promoting renewable energy production is clearly seen to trump the strict application of law.

54 *Kulovesi*, International Trade Disputes on Renewable Energy: Testing Ground for the Mutual Supportiveness of WTO Law and Climate Change Law, 23:3 Review of European Community and International Environmental Law (2014).

Thea Sveen
Researcher at the Scandinavian Institute of Maritime Law, Department of petroleum and energy law
t.b.sveen@jus.uio.no

The interaction between Article 192 and 194 TFEU: Renewable energy promotion with a predominant environmental purpose

Content

I. Introduction

If law is indeed the enterprise of subjecting human conduct to the governance of rules, we need to ask ourselves to what end? What is the purpose that we hope to achieve by doing so? The purpose is the yardstick for measuring the extent to which a law or a legal system is effective.[1]

Energy security and environmental protection have traditionally been perceived as two different concepts at the European and national level. With the increased knowledge and emphasis on climate change mitigation, conventional energy based on fossil fuels is no longer seen as a separate concept but inherently as the main reason for the increase in greenhouse gas emissions. Due to the enhanced emphasis on the development of a low-carbon economy as well as the reduction of European energy dependence on fossil fuels, energy security and environmental protection are increasingly moving closer within the European political and legal landscape.

In 2009, a specific energy provision was introduced into the TFEU. Article 194 TFEU is therefore a fairly new provision and there are still reasonable doubts concerning how the European Court of Justice (the Court) will interpret the wording and scope of the different elements encapsulated into this specific energy chapter. Coupled with the emphasis on climate change mitigation objectives, the fact still remains that secondary legislation regarding the promotion of renewable energy is based on Article 192 TFEU, the environmental provision, and not on Article 194 TFEU. In light of these developments, the energy and environmental provision have recently been recurring themes of the academic legal debate.[2]

However, if the explicit connection between energy security and environmental protection within the European legal landscape has been part of an overall strategy, the consequences of such a choice are multiplied at the national level, adding an extra dimension of confusion to the interpretation of both EU secondary and primary legislation.

---

1 *Cullinan*, The rule of Nature's law, in: Voigt (ed.), Rule of law for Nature, New Dimensions and Ideas in Environmental Law, (Cambridge University Press, 2014), p. 99.

2 See *Bjørnebye*, Investing in EU Energy Security: Exploring the Regulatory Approach to Tomorrow's Electricity Production, Energy and Environmental Law and Policy Series, Vol. 11/2010, Alphen aan den Rijn, (Kluwer Law International, 2010), *Talus*, EU Energy Law and Policy, (OUP, 2013), *de Sadeleer,* EU Environmental Law and the Internal Market (OUP, 2014); *Johnston/van der Marel*, Ad Lucem? Interpreting the New EU Energy provision and in particular the Meaning of Article 194(2) TFEU, European Energy and Environmental Law review, 2013: 22, pp. 181–199.

The question where Article 192 TFEU ends and Article 194 TFEU starts is certainly not clear from a legal perspective. This confusion may enhance the risks of misinterpretations regarding the purpose and spirit of primary and secondary legislation at the national level. In this lies the catch, notably the functioning and scope of the competences allocated to the European Union with regards to measures falling within the energy and within the environmental domain simultaneously. Further, this evolution may entail significant spill-over effects towards a sustainable European energy policy.[3]

The interpretation of EU law by the Court when energy related measures are coupled with a predominant environmental purpose both increases the discretion the European legislature if the measure is within the exclusive competence of the European Union and enables the Court to elevate their interpretation of both primary and secondary legislation by applying the principle of environmental protection more broadly on the other. Thus, the notion of a predominant environmental purpose and its scope are examined in cases where energy and environmental provisions directly or indirectly interact. In this context, the similarities and differences between the two primary law provisions will be examined. The second part will examine recent judgments of the Court when energy and environmental goals are intertwined.

II. Distinction and similarities between the energy and environmental provision of the Treaty

The objectives pursued in Article 191 TFEU are the following: the preservation, protection and improvement of the quality of the environment, the protection of human health, prudent and rational utilisation of natural resources, promotion of measures at international level to deal with regional or worldwide environmental problems and *in particular combating climate change*.[4] According to the Commission, "Articles 191 to 193 of the TFEU confirm and further specify EU competencies in the area of climate change."[5]

---

3 Functionalist and later neo-functionalist theory has identified spill-over effect where the dynamics of one policy area spills over to another. This is one of the core theories of European integration. For further reading, see *E. Haas*, Beyond the nation-State: functionalism and international organization (Stanford University Press, 1964).

4 My emphasis added, Article 192(2) TFEU is the vehicle in order to achieve these objectives.

5 Commission Staff Working Document, Executive Summary of the Impact Assessment accompanying the document Communication from the Commission to the European

There is no explicit reference to renewable energy promotion within the environmental provision itself. However, Article 192(2) (c) TFEU counteracts this by reiterating the measures mentioned in Article 194(2) TFEU second subparagraph.[6] As Article 194(1) (c) TFEU grants the EU competence in the area of the development of new and renewable forms of energy, Article 194(2) second subparagraph that the measures shall "not affect a Member State's right to determine the conditions for exploiting its energy resources, its choice between energy sources and the general structure of its energy supply" without prejudice to Article 192(2) TFEU where the Council may adopt decisions according to the special legislative procedure with unanimity after consulting the other EU bodies.[7]

Despite their significant impacts on the Member States' choices regarding energy mixes and energy policy in general, various acts regarding the fight against global warming fall under environmental policy and are adopted within this policy area. Indeed, as the environmental and energy legislation within the European Union becomes more detailed and more intertwined, it is hard to define where the European Union has not preempted Member State action. Consequently, the argument that shared competences might involve traits of an exclusive competence when exercised could be upheld within the context of environmental protection intertwined with energy policy goals.[8]

1. Shared competences

The very first Article of the TEU stipulates that "[t]he Member States confer competences to attain objectives they have in common".[9] This phrase could thus be argued to represent the direct translation of the relationship between competences and common objectives or interests within the European Union. As upheld by the Commission "when an objective has been recognized by the Union as being

Parliament, the Council, the European Economic and Social Committee and the Committee of the Regions A policy framework for climate and energy in the period from 2020 up to 2030, SWD(2014) 16 final, 22.1.2014, p. 13.

6 The fact that the conditions for exploiting the energy resources are not mentioned in Article 192(2) (c) TFEU has also been underlined by *Johnston/van der Marel (2013)* p. 196.

7 For an in-depth analysis of Article 194(2) second subparagraph see *Johnston/van der Marel*, Ad Lucem? Interpreting the New EU Energy Provision, and in particular the Meaning of Article 194(2) TFEU, European Energy and Environmental Law Review, 2013: 22, p. 192.

8 *Jaqué*, Droit institutionel de l'Union européenne, (Cours Dalloz, 7th ed. 2012), p. 156.

9 Article 1 TEU.

in the common interest of the EU Member States, it follows that it is an objective of common interest".[10] In this lies the understanding of the reason behind the allocation of competences to the European Union.

Energy and environment are, according to the TFEU shared competences and thereby adhere to the principles related to this particular competence in Article 2(2) TFEU and listed in Article 4(2) e) and i) TFEU respectively.[11]

As Member States and the European Union legislate in accordance with the principle of conferral, the explicit mentioning of the competences in the specific provisions related to energy and environment in the Treaty both enables and restricts EU action within the two respective areas. Article 2 (2) TFEU enables both the Union and the Member States to legislate and adopt legally binding acts within both energy and environment.[12]

Inherent to the character of shared competence, Member States are pre-empted to act as long as the European Union has acted on the matter in question, the density and scope of the detailed secondary framework therefore decrease the domains left to the Member States and it is ultimately the choice of legislation which "will determine the practical divide between Member State and EU competence".[13]

Thus, as environmental and energy legislation become more detailed, both within the Treaty itself and within the context of secondary legislation, this may ultimately enhance EU pre-emption over Member State action.

a) A new legal environment for energy

One of the elements which may enhance EU leverage after integrating environmental protection as an overriding EU principle is when measures are deemed to have a main predominant environmental purpose. This is also applicable in the field of energy policy where environmental objectives are directly or indirectly included

10 State aid SA 34947 (2013/C) (ex 2013/N) – United Kingdom Investment Contract for the Hinkley Point New Nuclear Power Station, Brussels, 18.12.2013, C(2013) 9073 final point 237.

11 Article 2(2) TFEU stipulates that "When the Treaties confer on the Union a competence shared with the Member States in a specific area, the Union and the Member States may legislate and adopt legally binding acts in that area. The Member States shall exercise their competence to the extent that the Union has not exercised its competence. The Member States shall again exercise their competence to the extent that the Union has decided to cease exercising its competence". Article 4(2) lit. e) and i) TFEU lists environment and energy as shared competences.

12 Article 2(2) TFEU.

13 *Craig*, The Lisbon Treaty: law, politics and Treaty Reform, (OUP, 2010), p. 171.

but it is certainly clear that the energy provision entails more environmental aims than the environmental provision defines energy related goals. Further, Article 11 TFEU and Article 37 of the Charter add to this calculation.[14]

Accordingly, no priority between the Union's environmental policy and its energy policy exists but "Article 194(1) TFEU provides that the Union's energy policy shall have regard to the need to preserve and improve the environment whereas Article 191(1) TFEU refers to the objective of combating climate change".[15] The introduction of a specific energy chapter has been part of a long process and "subsequent attempts to include a chapter on energy, during the negotiations on the Maastricht and Amsterdam Treaties ended in failure".[16] Although the Treaty of Maastricht sought a small change with the introduction of energy in its Article 3 § 1 a specific energy provision did not exist within the Treaty itself.[17] Hence, the development of a mature energy policy at the Treaty level was not feasible before Lisbon and the introduction of Article 194 TFEU.

Regarding the competences enshrined upon the Union, Member State sovereignty is not absolute and the energy component within the environmental provision need to be read in a consistent manner with regards to the other competences allocated to the Union.

As elaborated above, the caveat "without prejudice to the application of other provisions of the Treaties" indicates that the competence limit only applies to the extent to which the Member States have not yet transferred competences by other Treaty provisions.[18]

b) Defining the main predominant environmental purpose

The RES Directive was adopted on the basis of Article 192(2) TFEU and 114 TFEU. Therefore, it can be upheld that environmental protection is the main predominant purpose of this particular Directive. The Court has underlined that "if

---

14 *Morgera/Durán*, Article 37, in: Peers/Hervey/Kenner/Ward, The EU Charter of Fundamental Rights: A Commentary, (Hart Publishing, 2014) p. 983–1003. See also Scholz in this volume (Scholz, section IV 1 b).

15 Opinion AG Mazák in Case C-2/10 *Azienda Agro-Zootecnica Franchini sarl and Eolica di Altamura Srl v Regione Puglia* [2011] ECR I-6561, para. 47.

16 COM(2000) 769 final p. 12.

17 *C. Blumann*, Les compétences de l'Union européenne dans le domaine de l' énergie, Revue des. Affaires Européennes, 4, (2009–2010), p. 738.

18 *D. Fouquet et al.*, D3.1 Report: Potential areas of conflict of a harmonised RES support scheme with European Union Law (2012). http://www.res-policy-beyond2020.eu (accessed 13.03.2014) p. 18.

a measure is designed to pursue a two-fold purpose or has a twofold component, and if one of these is identifiable as the main or predominant purpose or component, the act must be based on the legal basis required by that main or predominant purpose or component".[19] Thus, the "rule of thumb" in order to avoid misinterpretations of the legal basis and its justification is to find "the centre of gravity of the act".[20]

On the one hand, questioning both the purpose and the aims to be achieved by promoting renewable energies is a legitimate question with regards to its legal basis. Applying the Court's guidance, it could be argued that the predominant environmental purpose is upheld within the directive itself by the definition of its legal basis. On the other hand, "[...] only a measure which simultaneously pursues several objectives that are *indissociably linked*, without one being secondary and indirect in relation to the other, may be founded on the various corresponding legal bases".[21]

Current case-law of the European courts could also be seen as a necessary tool and interpretation of the secondary legislation underlining protection of the environment as the predominant purpose or component. Nevertheless, different perspectives on this choice of legal basis have been put forward.

2. Predominant environmental purpose by default or by choice

The question is whether the legal basis for renewable energy promotion could be seen as an intended choice. Several scholars have pointed out that the environmental provision has been a legal basis by default. Consequently, "[...] where an environmental measure also only incidentally concerns energy goals and has such effects upon these Member States interests, then the default legal basis will be Article 192 TFEU."[22] Further, the environmental provision as a legal basis has also been attributed to the previous lack of an explicit EU energy competence:

Given the absence from the former EC Treaty of a chapter specifically dedicated to energy policy, certain measures promoting renewable energy were adopted on the basis of Article 175 EC (Art. 192 TFEU). The former absence from the Treaties

19 Opinion of AG Mengozzi Case C-490/10 *Parliament v Council* [2012] para. 41.
20 *De Sadeleer*, EU Environmental Law and the Internal Market, (OUP, 2014), p. 151.
21 Opinion of AG Mengozzi Case C-490/10 *Parliament v Council* [2012] para. 42.
22 *Johnston/van der Marel*, Ad Lucem? Interpreting the New EU Energy Provision, and in particular the Meaning of Article 194(2) TFEU, European Energy and Environmental Law Review, October 2013, p. 192.

of a chapter specifically dedicated to energy policy, certain measures promoting renewable energy were adopted on the basis of the environmental provision.[23]

The case law of the European courts has underlined the protection of the environment as the predominant purpose or component of the promotion of renewable energies.[24] The legal basis of the RES Directive is still Article 192(2) TFEU and not Article 194(2) TFEU. At a first glance, the difference between the provisions is not that striking. However, a closer examination identifies some key elements which distinguishes them and brings forward the predominant environmental purpose of renewable energy promotion. It might seem that Article 192(2) TFEU is not a legal basis by default but rather a strategic choice. Further, if energy and environmental concerns are increasingly becoming intertwined, the single legal basis of the energy efficiency directive demonstrate that even if it pursues two aims such as energy and environment, energy is identifiable as the main one, whereas environment is merely incidental and the directive founded on the single legal basis (Article 194(2) TFEU), underlining that the energy provision covers sufficiently the main or predominant aim or component of the secondary legislation in question.[25]

a) Similarities underlining the main predominant environmental purpose

Advocate General Mengozzi argued that Article 194 TFEU is a "provision laid down specifically to regulate European Union policy in the energy sector, and constitutes the general reference point for that policy".[26]. However, if energy has been a national prerogative, environmental protection follows a different logic in parallel to the polluter pays principle as well as the principle that pollution should be rectified at its source. In the overall European context, "the protection of the environment does not require a purely national understanding but has a European dynamic, in particular when faced with climate change mitigation". Hence, it is more than reasonable to believe that environmental protection and its subsequent legal framework is indeed better placed within an overreaching European logic

23 *De Sadeleer*, EU Environmental Law and the Internal Market, (OUP, 2014), p. 136.

24 Case C-573/12 *Ålands Vindkraft AB v Energimyndigheten* and Joined Cases C-204 & 208/12 *Essent Belgium NV*, not yet reported.

25 Case C-490/10 *Parliament v Council* [2012] para. 45. ECR not yet reported.

26 Opinion of AG Mengozzi in Case C-490/10 *Parliament v Council* [2012], para. 23.

which enables the legislator to act without directly applying the energy provision as measures do only incidentally interact with Article 194 TFEU.[27]

In addition, the RES Directive stipulates that "[t]he coherence between the objectives of this Directive and the Community's *other environmental legislation* should be ensured".[28] The wording of this preamble does indeed strengthen the hypothesis that renewable energy promotion is an integrated part of the Union's overall environmental legislation. This is why the question concerning the actual and proper positioning of renewable energy promotion in the primary EU law legal landscape has been raised and still continues to intrigue scholars and practitioners alike.

The case law of the European courts has underlined that the protection of the environment with its predominant purpose or component enables promotion of renewable energies specific derogations in the name of environmental protection.[29] A predominant environmental purpose is demonstrated also in light of derogations applicable to the energy provision itself and the environmental concerns therefore strengthened within this particular provision and in a broader internal market context.

As explained by Johnston and van der Marel, "[t]he preservation and improvement of the environment is, together with the functioning of the internal market, one of the two aims of Article 194 TFEU. *This means that a derogating measure which does not achieve a higher level of environmental protection is contrary to both of the objectives of Article 194 TFEU*, since by definition a derogating measure will also be an obstacle to the functioning of the internal market".[30]

b) Differences reflected in secondary legislation

In particular, the differences of the two provisions are made clear regarding the choice of the legal basis secondary legislation regarding energy efficiency and renewable energy promotion. The wording of the energy efficiency directive to "promote energy efficiency" in paragraph c), is also the same wording as within the

---

27 Opinion AG Bot in Joined Cases C-204 & 208/12 *Essent Belgium NV v Vlaame Reguleringsinstantie voor de Elekticiteits – en Gasmarkt*, not yet reported, para. 110.

28 RES Directive, recital 44.

29 Case C-573/12 *Ålands Vindkraft AB v Energimyndigheten* and Joined Cases C-204 & 208/12 *Essent Belgium NV v Vlaame Reguleringsinstantie voor de Elekticiteits – en Gasmarkt*, not yet reported.

30 *Johnston/van der Marel*, Ad Lucem? Interpreting the New EU Energy Provision, and in particular the Meaning of Article 194 (2) TFEU, European Energy and Environmental Law Review, October 2013, p. 189, my emphasis added.

context of promoting "the development of new and renewable forms of energy" within the same paragraph. Both directives thus maintain a direct connection with the wording of the energy provision of the Treaty. Nevertheless, the energy efficiency directive aimed to "establish a *common framework* to promote energy efficiency in the Union".[31] This is reiterated in the Directive itself.[32] However, such a common framework is indeed not the aim with regards to support schemes enabling the promotion of renewable energy at a national level. In addition, energy efficiency also includes the most efficient use of fossil fuels.

Although it may seem like the respective aims of the RES Directive are tailor-made for Article 194 TFEU, the legal basis is not questioned in the revision process in 2012 despite of the argumentation put forward that "[...] energy measures aiming at preventing climate change should be adopted by virtue of both Articles 192(1) and 194(2) TFEU."[33]

By ensuring reference both to the environment and the internal market, the communication from the Commission underlined that "the primary objective [of the Directive] is the protection of the environment and the functioning of the internal market. This proposal is therefore based on Articles 192(1) and 114 of the Treaty on the Functioning of the European Union" and no explicit reference to Article 194(2) TFEU was made.[34] Whether this situation will persist or whether a dual legal basis will be suggested is therefore a future question for further analysis.

III. Enhanced leverage with a predominant environmental purpose

Environmental protection as an overriding norm within the context of the interpretation of both primary and secondary legislation is encapsulated within

31 COM(2011) 370 final, Proposal for a Directive of the European Parliament and of the Council on energy efficiency and repealing Directives 2004/8/EC and 2006/32/EC p. 5.

32 Article 1 Directive 2012/27 of the European Parliament and of the Council of 25 October 2012 on energy efficiency, amending Directives 2009/125/EC and 2010/30/EU and repealing Directives 2004/8/EC and 2006/32/EC, OJ L 315/1 14.11.2012, my emphasis added.

33 *De Sadeleer*, EU Environmental Law and the Internal Market, (OUP, 2014), p. 136.

34 Proposal for a directive of the European Parliament and of the Council amending Directive 98/70/EC relating to the quality of petrol and diesel fuels and amending Directive 2009/28/EC on the promotion of the use of energy from renewable sources COM(2012) 595 final p. 5.

the Treaties.[35] From this author's view, the understanding of EU law cannot only be acquired from the wordings of the provisions but entails a larger teleological perspective. The Treaty itself, however, leaves renewable energy promotion stuck in the middle between the environmental provision and the energy provision through Article 194(2) and 192(2) (c) TFEU. As a consequence, a space of legal uncertainty with regards to the competences of the EU and member States respectively has been created.

However, a rather wishful argumentation is that Article 192(2) TFEU could be perceived as an intended choice, enabling the European Court to argue both in favour of exhaustive harmonisation where this is applicable without stepping on Article 194(2) TFEU's toes. Further, this enables a more consistent argumentation with regards to the derogations of the territorial restrictions of national support schemes in the name of environmental protection since this is in a European common interest.

Ålands Vindkraft and the *Essent* cases[36] have in particular fueled the argumentation both in favour and against the interpretation of Member States flexibility to determine both *if* or alternatively *to what extent* their national support schemes apply to energy from renewable sources produced in other Member States.[37] On the one hand, the interdependency of energy and environment seems to steer the Court in its interpretation to argue against derogations if energy related concerns do not benefit a higher protection of the environment. On the other hand, derogations are more easily justified if energy policy related measures may improve the protection of the environment. These arguments will be exemplified below by two recent judgments of the General Court and the European Court of Justice respectively. This further strengthens the argumentation that the environmental provision remains the best choice in order to elevate environmental protection and balance it against other concerns, such as the functioning of the internal market.

---

35 The emphasis on sustainable development and protection of the environment are also mentioned in Article 11 TFEU, Article 21 TEU as well as Article 37 of the Charter.

36 Case C-573/12 *Ålands Vindkraft AB v Energimyndigheten* [2014] and Joined Cases C-204 & 208/12 *Essent Belgium NV v Vlaamse Reguleringsinstantie voor de Elekticiteits – en Gasmarkt,* not yet reported.

37 For detailed analysis, see the contribution in this volume by Scholz regarding territorial restrictions and national renewable energy promotion schemes, *Scholz*, section VI 2.

1. An intended choice of legal basis

More than being the vehicle for fulfilling EU environmental policy objectives and representing the legal basis for the RES Directive, the environmental provision as a legal basis for secondary legislations enhances the environmental purpose of the promotion of renewable energy. Article 194 TFEU is argued to have "only incrementally changed the limited EU role in steering national energy policies directly. The EU impact on the national energy mix is predominantly indirect, yet powerful."[38]

As argued above, Article 192 TFEU could be seen as an intended or rather pragmatic choice in order to strengthen the environmental dimension of renewable energy and should continue to do so when environment and energy are becoming increasingly intertwined at the legal and political level. It is precisely this indirect impact that is crucial for the understanding on the way in which the EU legislature navigates through environmental policy objectives avoiding a direct confrontation with Article 194(2) TFEU. Article 192(2) (c) TFEU which creates a circular composition enabling a strong emphasis also in matters regarding energy where the "measures referred to [...] imply the involvement of the European institutions in the area of energy policy".[39] Even if a specific energy provision has been included within the Treaty, this will not exclude the application of the environmental provision.[40]

a) *Exhaustive harmonisation*

Republic of Poland v European Commission has indeed shed some light, but not enlightened, the current situation where both environmental and energy policies are intertwined.[41] The Commission was allowed to adopt under secondary legislation a "fully-harmonised implementing measure" based on Article 10a of

38 *Calliess/Hey*, Multilevel Energy Policy in the EU: Paving the Way for Renewables? Jounral for European Environmental planning law, (Martinus Nijhoff Publishers, 2013), p. 88.

39 Case T-370/11 *Republic of Poland v Commission* [2013], not yet reported para. 18.

40 *Fouquet et al.*, D3.1 Report: Potential areas of conflict of a harmonised RES support scheme with European Union Law (2012), http://www.res-policy-beyond2020.eu (last accessed 13.03.2014) p. 12.

41 See also Johnston in this volume concerning the impact of the new EU Commission guidelines on State aid for environmental protection and energy on the promotion of renewable energies, *Johnston,* section IV 4).

Directive 2003/87/EC.[42] The Commission used natural gas as the reference point for determining the benchmarks related to product, heat and fuel. This in turn made Poland argue that such an approach would "redirect companies towards purchasing gas technology, as a consequence of the contested decision, would increase the natural gas needs of the State concerned, disrupt its energy balance and force it to redefine its overall energy policy".[43] The Republic of Poland further argued that "Member States never assigned exclusive jurisdiction to the European Union regarding the matter referred to in the second subparagraph of Article 194(2) TFEU".[44]

The legal basis for the directive enabling such an implementation was Article 192(2) TFEU and not Article 194(2) TFEU, a situation quite similar to the legal basis of the RES Directive. The factor triggering the reasoning of the General Court was that the alleged infringement of Article 194(2) TFEU by the Republic of Poland read in conjunction with 192(2) (c) TFEU could not be upheld, as the contested decision was not adopted on the basis of Article 194(2) TFEU.[45] If the timing was not right due to the alleged infringement of a non-existing energy provision at the moment the decision was adopted, the case could nevertheless be useful with regards to the relationship between energy and environment at the European level.

The Republic of Poland alleged a breach of the second subparagraph of Article 194(2) TFEU arguing that "measures adopted in the context of other policies cannot affect that right".[46] However, the allegation of competence creep within an exhaustively harmonised area was not upheld:

[...] it is true that, under the second subparagraph of Article 194(2) TFEU, measures established in accordance with the procedure laid down in the first subparagraph of that paragraph and necessary to achieve the policy objectives of the European Union in the area of energy, referred to in para. 1 of that article, cannot affect the right of a Member State to determine the conditions for exploiting its energy resources, its choice between different energy sources and the general structure of its energy supply. However, there is no reason to suppose that the

42 Case T-370/11 Republic of Poland v Commission, not yet reported, para. 2. Exhaustive harmonisation would certainly not be the case in the context of renewable energy promotion as maintained by the Court in both *Åland* and *Essent*.

43 Case T-370/11 *Republic of Poland v Commission,* not yet reported, para. 10.

44 Case T- 370/11 *Republic of Poland v Commission* [2013], not yet reported, para. 16.

45 This argumentation goes in line with the other observation and comments made by Johnston in this volume, *Johnston*, section IV 4.

46 Case T 370/11 *Republic of Poland v Commission* [2013], not yet reported para. 16.

second subparagraph of Article 194(2) TFEU establishes a general prohibition to assign that right that is applicable in European Union policy in the area of the environment [...]. On the one hand, Article 194 TFEU is a general provision which relates solely to the energy sector and, consequently, delineates a sectoral competence [...]. On the other hand, it should be noted that the second subparagraph of Article 194(2) TFEU expressly refers to point (c) of the first subparagraph of Article 192(2) TFEU. Indeed, the second subparagraph Article 194(2) TFEU provides that the prohibition on affecting the right of a Member State to determine the conditions for exploiting its energy resources, its choice between different energy sources and the general structure of its energy supply applies without prejudice to point (c) of the first subparagraph of Article 192(2) TFEU. While it is true that that latter provision is only procedural in nature, it none the less provides specific rules relating to the environment policy of the European Union. It follows that the right referred to in the second subparagraph of Article 194(2) TFEU is not applicable in the present case, *since the contested decision constitutes an action taken by the European Union within the framework of its environment policy.*[47]

b) Harmonisation not intended by the legislature

Whereas *Poland v. Commission* demonstrated a case where an area had been exhaustively harmonised on the European level, notably through setting benchmarks in the ETS sector prior to the adoption of a specific energy provision, the same reasoning cannot be reproduced with regards to renewable energy promotion support schemes. The choice of legal basis seems to underline whether the secondary legislation has a stronger emphasis on the internal market:

EU measures establishing environmental targets and introducing instruments not directly affecting or regulating trade of goods or services have been based on the environmental competence of Article 192(2) TFEU. Apparently, trade in emission allowances was not considered an internal market issue, but the environmental objective prevailed. On the other hand, the chosen legal basis of Article 114 TFEU for sustainability criteria on biofuels under the RES Directive confirms the relevance of the internal market in the case of direct impacts on trade in goods. However, since the introduction of the new energy competence, this one has been

47 Case T-370/11 *Republic of Poland v Commission* [2013], not yet reported para. 17, emphasis added.

used, both for market as for security of supply objectives, thus confirming that this is not the appropriate basis and applies as *lex specialis.*[48]

Environmental protection enables derogation from the internal market rules within Article 194 TFEU and indirectly gives the European Court of Justice a possibility to enhance the EU leverage on this matter. However, this is done in two contrasting ways. First, the RES Directive has been interpreted as a measure where to ensure the proper functioning of the various national support schemes in reaching the targets and the EU legislature thus induced a possibility of territorial limitation with regards to national mandatory targets.[49] If "any prohibition on territorial restrictions would cause the Member States to lose control over their energy mix"[50], the allegation of an implicit attack on Member States energy sovereignty rights by using EU environmental policy and subsequently used Article 192(2) (c) TFEU as a counterbalance could be argued to follow the same logic as in Republic of Poland v. Commission but this within an area of exhaustive harmonisation. Not surprisingly, Yves Bot's reasoning also underlines the potential increase of EU leverage on environmental protection indirectly or directly related to energy policy via the vehicle of the environmental provision. By adding that Article 192(2) (c) TFEU "empowers the European Union to adopt, in the context of its environmental policy, 'measures significantly affecting a Member State's choice between different energy sources and the general structure of its energy supply" it is strikingly clear that the Court is aware of this interaction.[51] In addition, territorial restrictions were explicitly mentioned with regards to Article 192(2) TFEU second subparagraph:

That argument [prohibition on territorial restrictions] does not seem to me to be any more valid than the previous arguments. Whilst it is clear from the second subparagraph of Article 194(2) TFEU that the European Union's energy policy is intended to preserve freedom of choice as regards national energy mixes, without prejudice to Article 192(2) (c) TFEU, such energy policy decisions may nevertheless be affected by measures adopted by the European Union in the context of its

---

48 *Fouquet et al.*, D3.1 Report: Potential areas of conflict of a harmonised RES support scheme with European Union Law (2012), http://www.res-policy-beyond2020.eu (last accessed 13.03.2014) p. 23.

49 Case C-573/12 *Ålands Vindkraft AB v Energimyndigheten,* not yet reported, paras. 40 and 49.

50 Opinion AG Bot Case C-573/12 *Ålands Vindkraft AB v Energimyndigheten* [2014] not yet reported, para. 103.

51 Footnote of the AG's Bot Opinion Case C-573/12 *Ålands Vindkraft AB v Energimyndigheten* [2014] not yet reported, para. 104.

environmental policy, as is demonstrated by the RES Directive itself, which, by laying down mandatory targets for green energy consumption in each Member State, necessarily exerts an influence on the composition of their respective energy mixes."[52]

Further, "[...] since, in particular, EU law has not harmonised the national support schemes for green electricity, it is possible in principle for Member States to limit access to such schemes to green electricity production located in their territory".[53]

Although Arts. 194 and 191 TFEU are only used as indirect references in *the Ålands Vindkraft* case, it is clear that the Court acknowledges their importance for the question at hand. As stated in the *Ålands Vindkraft* case, "[i]t is also clear from Article 194(1) (c) TFEU that the development of renewable energy is one of the objectives that must guide EU energy policy".[54]

2. The unresolved future legal question

When faced with a Treaty provision with multiple layers and which seems also to have multiple functions, the scope and content of Article 192 TFEU in the context of renewable energy promotion directly interacts with both Article 194(2) and 107(3) TFEU at a primary law level. Support schemes are deemed necessary in order to enhance the promotion of renewable energy within the European Union and all address a market failure being the most important criteria of allocating State aid.

The perspective on State aid as an inherent part of the internal market and not separate from it, elevates environmental and energy to a more coherent understanding of the functioning of EU law.[55] Article 2(1) TFEU should be read as the first basic principle regarding the character of an exclusive competence within the EU where only the Union may legislate and adopt legally binding acts.[56]

Within this context, "the consequences of inclusion within this category are severe: the Member States have no autonomous legislative competence and they cannot adopt any legally binding act".[57] Nevertheless, the newly adopted mandatory

52 AG Bot Case C-573/12 *Ålands Vindkraft AB v Energimyndighete,* not yet reported, para. 104.

53 *Ibid.* paras. 93 and 94.

54 Case C-573/12 *Ålands Vindkraft AB v Energimyndighete,* not yet reported, para. 81.

55 *De Cecco*, State aid and the European Economic Constitution, (Hart Publishing Oxford, 2013) p. 31.

56 Article 2(1) TFEU.

57 *Craig*, The Lisbon Treaty: law, politics and Treaty Reform, (OUP, 2010), p. 160.

target of renewable energy consumption at the European level is increasingly becoming subject to the energy and environmental State aid guidelines. Further, this is triggered by the Commission's discretion regarding a European common interest.

a) *Mandatory targets in the context of Article 192(2) TFEU*

According to *Talus*, "[...] the new energy title should *a priori* not restrict Member State's choices with respect to energy sources."[58] The choice of legal basis is particularly relevant in the context of the mandatory renewable energy targets and has been argued to "clearly restrict the right of the Member States to decide on their energy mix [...] was adopted under the wrong legal basis, and is therefore in conflict with the Treaty, provided of course that a requirement that approximately half the national electricity production be from renewable energy sources instead of nuclear, coal, natural gas, or other options considered to "significantly affect" the right of a Member State to choose between different sources of energy".[59] Clearly, the promotion of renewable energy steers the Member States in adopting measures regarding their energy policies.

But if these policies are seen within the context of the environmental policy of the European Union, the discretion becomes even bigger at the European level concerning both derogations to the internal market rules as well as measures enabling an exhaustive harmonisation as seen in the *Poland v. Commission* and *Ålands Vindkraft*.

The most interesting point is that mandatory targets are referred to when secondary legislation is adopted by the environmental provision whereas indicative targets still seem to be the most appropriate measure when dealing with secondary legislation adopted by virtue of the energy provision. This further gets more complicated when the mandatory target is elevated to become a binding target at the EU level.[60] Nevertheless, it is probably the exclusive competence of the Union which will ultimately determine the details regarding the way in which this target should be achieved. The compatibility of State aid is after the adoption of the new energy and environmental State aid guidelines based on Article 107(3) (c) TFEU. Such aid is defined as "aid to facilitate the development of certain economic activities or of certain economic areas, where such aid does not adversely affect trading conditions to an extent contrary to the common interest". Prior to the adaptation

58 *Talus*, EU Energy Law and Policy, (OUP, 2013), p. 179.
59 *Talus*, EU Energy Law and Policy. (OUP, 2013), p. 180.
60 European Council Conclusions of 23/24 October 2014, EUCO 169/14, point 3.

of the new guidelines, a direct reference was also made concerning Article 107(3) (b), which is different in nature as it encompasses "aid to promote the execution of an important project of common European interest or to remedy a serious disturbance in the economy of a Member State".

If the view that "[…] competition law will not on its own resolve the problems of pollution, as it is nothing more than an instrument in the service of environmental policy"[61] could be upheld, the new State-aid guidelines are nevertheless presented as being a "key contribution to achieving the EU's energy and climate objectives for 2020 and strengthening cross-border energy flows."[62]

Further, the projects deemed to be in a European common interest under Article 107(3) (b) TFEU *"must contribute in a concrete, exemplary and identifiable manner to the Community interest in the field of environmental protection, such as being of great importance for the environmental strategy of the European Union."*[63] As held by de Cecco, "[i]t is clear from the treaty provisions, from secondary legislation and from the Court's case law that, to be regarded as justified, State aid should contribute towards the achievement of an EU objective".[64]

In this authors view, a mandatory EU binding target of renewable energy consumption may fall within the category of an important common interest. It is particularly in the context of the newly adopted environmental and energy State aid guidelines that this element comes to the fore. After the entry into force of the Treaty on the Functioning of the European Union and the explicit mentioning of EU competences, it has been held that this "very creation of categories of competence […] inevitably means that there will be problems of demarcating borderlines between the different categories. Such problems can arise in demarcating the line between exclusive and shared competence".[65]

---

61 *De Sadeleer*, EU Environmental Law and the Internal Market, (OUP, 2014), p. 467.

62 European Commission Press Release, State aid: Commission consults on draft rules for State support in energy and environmental field, IP/13/1282, Brussels 18 December 2013, p. 1.

63 Community guidelines 2008/C 82/01 on State aid for environmental protection [2008] OJ C82/1 point. 147 a) and b) my emphasis added.

64 *De Cecco*, State aid and the European Economic Constitution, (Hart Publishing Oxford, 2013), p. 52.

65 *Craig*, The Lisbon Treaty: law, politics and Treaty Reform, (OUP, 2010), p. 160.

b) *Binding European target and the importance of a European common interest*

Article 107(3) (c) TFEU represents "the most significant of the discretionary exceptions".[66] Article 107(3) TFEU explicitly introduces a safe-guard clause, leaving much discretion to the European Commission in asserting whether the measure in question "may" be compatible with the internal market.[67] This author argues that it is through the lenses of Article 107(3) (b) and Article 107(3) (c) TFEU that the definition concerning the way in which the leverage between the environmental and energy provision will be achieved and defined.[68] It should thus not be surprising that the energy efficiency target remains indicative target of at least 27 % is not subject to an EU overall binding target.[69] More importantly,

[t]hese targets will be achieved while fully respecting Member States' freedom to determine their energy mix. Targets will not be translated into nationally binding targets. Individual Member States are free to set their own higher national targets".[70] As an EU target of at least 27 % is set for the share of renewable energy consumed in the EU in 2030 is set and will be binding at EU level, Member States need to deliver collectively the EU target without preventing more ambitious national targets, *in line with the State aid guidelines.*[71]

This may possibly explain the reason why the enhanced emphasis of renewable energy consumption within the context of an EU binding target increases the discretionary derogations in the name of a common interest when faced with Article 107(3) TFEU. The assessment of the primary law provisions with regards to Article 107(3) (c) TFEU clearly allocates the environmental common interest of decarbonisation to Article 191 TFEU while Article 194 TFEU is assessed in view of enhanced security of energy supply. According to the Commission, "[...] Art. 191 TFEU establishes that the preservation, improvement and protection of the environment must be regarded as objectives of EU policy".[72]

---

66 *De Burca/Craig*, EU Law: text, cases and materials, (OUP, 4th ed. 2007), p. 1095.

67 *Ibid.* p. 1092–1093.

68 This is also in line with the argumentation by Johnston in his contribution to this volume regarding *the quasi legislative* nature of the EEAG Guidelines. For detailed analysis, *Johnston*, section IV 2 b) bb).

69 European Council Conclusions of 23/24 October 2014, EUCO 169/14, point 3.

70 *Ibid.*

71 *Ibid.*

72 State aid SA. 34947 (2013/C) (ex 2013/N) – United Kingdom Investment Contract for the Hinkley Point C New Nuclear Power Station, Brussels, 18.12.2013, C(2013) 9073 final point. 240.

Pursuant to Article 194 TFEU, the Commission claimed that "in the context of the establishment and functioning of the internal market, the Union policy on energy shall aim *inter alia* to ensure security of energy supply in the Union [...] an objective which the Court has also recognised as being an overriding reason in the public interest".[73] The following cumulative criteria are to be met:

> The project must contribute in a concrete, clear and identifiable manner to one or more Union objectives and must have a significant impact on competitiveness of the Union, sustainable growth, addressing societal challenges or value creation across the Union.
>
> The project must represent an important contribution to the Union's objectives, for instance by being of major importance for the Europe 2020 strategy, the European Research Area, the European strategy for KETs , the Energy Strategy for Europe, the 2030 framework for climate and energy policies, the European Energy Security Strategy, the Electronics Strategy for Europe, the Trans-European Transport and Energy networks [....]
>
> The project must normally involve more than one Member State and its benefits must not be confined to the financing Member States, but extend to a *wide part of the Union*. The benefits of the project must be clearly defined in a concrete and identifiable manner [...].[74]

IV. Conclusion

The renewed debate on the actual place of renewable energy within both primary and secondary EU law and the constant evolution of EU legislation in the context of renewable energy promotion invite scholars to reflect on the actual and correct place occupied by renewable energy. The main argument is that the promotion of renewable energy is best guaranteed when its predominant environmental purpose is pursued. Further, the discretion of the European Courts and of the European legislature in areas where energy and environment are combined is enhanced due to a predominant environmental purpose.

If the RES Directive is based and will continue to be based on the environmental provision, there is no doubt that the aim and spirit of this secondary legislation directly reflects the aims and spirit of the primary law provision which is environmental protection.

The connection between Article 107(3) (b) (c) TFEU and Article 191 and 194 TFEU in the context of decarbonisation and security of supply as a common

---

73 *Ibid.* point. 248.

74 Communication from the Commission, Criteria for the analysis of the compatibility with the internal market of State aid to promote the execution of important projects of common European interest, 2014/C 188/02, point. 3.2.1.

objective is deemed to become more explicit. The common objectives of Article 191 and 194 TFEU are used in order to underpin the Commission's assessment regarding whether the measure contributes to a common European interest. Having in mind the increased emphasis on streamlining the perception of Member States′ support schemes and promotion of renewable energy sources as well as underlining its predominant environmental purpose, Article 107(3) (b) and 107(3) (c) TFEU may in the future become useful tools in order reflect on the actual definition of a common environmental interest and strengthen the leverage sought by the European Union through the vehicle of Article 192(2) TFEU. Nevertheless, the shared competence requires unanimity in the Council according to the special legislative procedure but the discretion of the Commission will possibly be used in order to reach the 2030 targets within the area of an exclusive competence. Where important projects of European Common Interest (IPECI) were previously deemed necessary to extend to the Union *as a whole*, the definition now consists of benefits which should extend to a *wide part of the Union*, and thus includes a narrower definition under the European Commission scrutiny and enabling more projects to fall within this category.[75]

By transforming the mandatory national targets into a binding EU target, it could be argued that the new energy and environmental State aid guidelines will be the reference point in order to achieve this goal within the 2030 framework by enhancing the use of both Article 107(3) (b) and (c) TFEU. The guidelines related to Article 107(3) (b) TFEU have been adopted at a very specific moment, within a specific international context and underlines the importance of Commission derogatory discretion to the general prohibition of State aid in the intersection between the energy and environmental primary law provisions.

75 Communication from the Commission, Criteria for the analysis of the compatibility with the internal market of State aid to promote the execution of important projects of common European interest, COM(2014) 3290, point 16.

Carsten König
Researcher at Enreg Institute of Energy and Regulatory Law, Berlin
koenig@enreg.eu

How congestion management rules challenge the development of an integrated offshore electricity infrastructure in the North Sea

Content

I. Introduction[1]

The existing electricity infrastructure in the North Sea consists of undersea cables and a number of offshore wind farms which is steadily increasing.[2] By the end of 2013, more than 4,000 MW of offshore wind capacity had been installed in the North Sea.[3] The UK is particularly successful in promoting offshore wind energy, followed by Denmark and Germany.[4] Undersea cables either connect offshore wind farms to onshore electricity grids[5] or they connect onshore electricity grids to each other, i.e. they serve as so called interconnectors.[6]

In the forthcoming years and decades, the existing electricity infrastructure is deemed to undergo radical changes. In 2009, the North Sea coastal States formed the North Seas Countries' Offshore Grid Initiative (NSCOGI) which aims to facilitate the coordinated development of an offshore electricity grid in the North Sea. The initiative is supported by the energy ministries in the respective States, the regulators and the transmission system operators as well as by the European Commission. It seeks to maximize the efficient and economic use of renewable energy resources in addition to infrastructure investments.[7]

In order to achieve these goals, technical studies suggest the development of an integrated offshore electricity grid infrastructure.[8] An integrated offshore grid in the North Sea would contribute to a high degree of security of supply, promote

---

1 The author thanks Professor Dr. Dr. Dr. h.c. Franz Jürgen Säcker and Professor Dr. Lydia Scholz with whom he conducted the study "The Regulatory Framework for an Offshore Electricity Grid in the North Sea – Barriers and Proposals How to Overcome Them" (original title: Der regulierungsrechtliche Rahmen für ein Offshore-Stromnetz in der Nordsee – Hemmnisse und Vorschläge für deren Überwindung).

2 EWEA, The European offshore wind industry – key trends and statistics 2013, January 2014; EWEA, The European offshore wind industry – key trends and statistics, first half 2014, July 2014.

3 EWEA, The European offshore wind industry – key trends and statistics 2013, January 2014, p. 11.

4 EWEA, The European offshore wind industry – key trends and statistics 2013, January 2014, p. 11.

5 Connection lines are built as single lines or clusters, but are always national in scope. So far, there are no cross-border connections or connections to more than one coast.

6 Infra, section II.

7 Http://www.benelux.int/nl/kernthemas/energie/nscogi-2012-report/ (last visited 13/11/2014).

8 3E, Offshore Electricity Grid Infrastructure in Europe, Final Report, October 2011.

cross-border trade in electricity and allow for a better integration of large quantities of electricity generated from offshore-wind energy.

However, its development is technically challenging and requires massive investments. Thus, an integrated offshore grid can only become reality on the basis of a close cooperation between all relevant parties and undertakings.[9]

II. The important role of interconnectors

Evidently, the structure of an integrated offshore grid would not be as complex as the one of modern onshore grids. It can probably best be compared with the grid of a sparsely-populated country. It would consist of very few highly interconnected subsystems in and between offshore wind farms close to each other, and some connection cables over longer distances.[10] The degree of interconnection would be much smaller than it typically is in European onshore grids. However, it would still be sufficient to gain the benefits of interconnection, i.e. a multiplication of transportation routes, safeguarding a high degree of security of supply and the opportunity to exchange electricity between national markets in order to foster competition.

1. New interconnectors

Interconnectors, i.e. subsea cables that connect national electricity grids with each other, are to play a decisive role in the development of an integrated offshore grid. They are important for cross-border trading because they enable electricity exchanges between neighbouring markets. Several new interconnectors are to be constructed in the forthcoming years, among them the *Cobra Cable* between the Netherlands and Denmark, a new *Channel Cable* between the UK and France and the *Nordlink* cable between Germany and Norway. Interconnectors to Norway are especially attractive because of its vast potential for energy storage.

---

9 *Säcker/König/Scholz*, Der regulierungsrechtliche Rahmen für ein Offshore-Stromnetz in der Nordsee, (P. Lang, 2014), p. 125 ff.

10 3E, Offshore Electricity Grid Infrastructure in Europe, Final Report, October 2011, p. 12 ff.

Figure 1: Interconnector development (sketch).

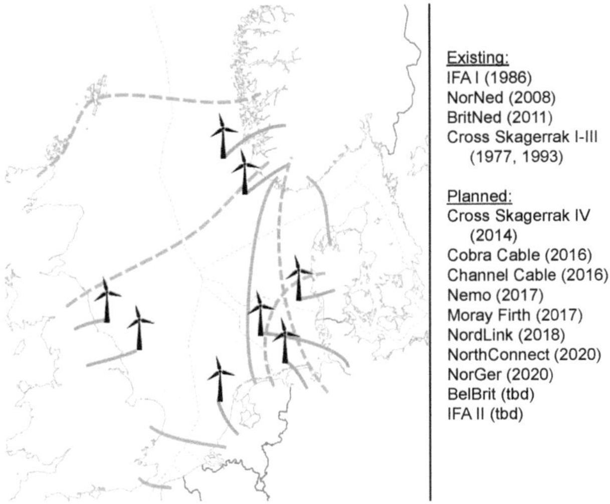

The construction of new interconnectors will contribute significantly to the integration of electricity infrastructure in the North Sea. Interconnectors better connect national grid systems and thereby allow for the integration of electricity markets. From a technical point of view, it is also possible to connect interconnectors with connection cables or even with each other. This makes interconnectors the 'backbone' of an integrated offshore grid.

2. Two models

New interconnectors will also provide for new opportunities to connect offshore wind farms to the grid. Already today, transmission system operators explore the possibility to directly connect wind farms to interconnectors. The most prominent example is the *Cobra Cable*, an interconnector that is to be constructed between the Netherlands and Denmark and shall be completed by the end of 2016. At a later stadium, the investors seek to directly connect offshore wind farms to the *Cobra Cable*. In technical studies, this model is called a tee-in connection.[11] Another technical option currently explored is the so called hub-to-hub connection.[12] According to this approach the interconnector does not connect national

11 3E, Offshore Electricity Grid Infrastructure in Europe, Final Report, October 2011, p. 10.
12 *Ibid.*

onshore grids, as it is the usual way, but it connects the hubs of two different offshore wind farms.

Figure 2: tee-in connection (left), hub-to-hub connection (right).

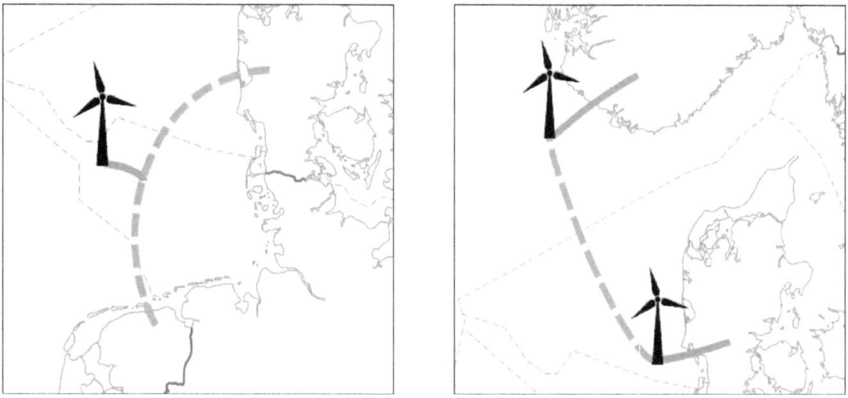

Both models have the advantage that they allow to use infrastructure for two purposes at the same time. In case of strong winds, the whole transmission capacity can be used to transport electricity from the wind farms to the electricity grids onshore.

However, if there is only little electricity generation from offshore wind farms, the existing cables can be used for cross-border electricity exchanges. Thus, they contribute to market integration and low wholesale prices, at least in markets that are typically confronted with high prices. Such a 'double purpose infrastructure' allows for an efficient and economic use of available capacities. From a technical point of view it is therefore considered highly beneficial.

The innovative use of offshore transmission infrastructure could, however, raise a number of legal questions. The current frameworks both on the EU and the national level do not stipulate specifically how offshore infrastructure is to be used. Yet, if the general rules for electricity transmission infrastructure are applied, the result is not free from conflicts – as it will be demonstrated in the following section.

III. Regulatory regimes

Legal provisions on the development of offshore electricity infrastructure are primarily to be found in national laws. The North Sea coastal States apply very different concepts to incentivise the construction of offshore wind farms and their timely connection to onshore electricity grids.[13] Since offshore electricity generation and transmission are relatively new technologies, there are very few harmonised rules that apply. The Third Energy Package, for instance, does not at all cover offshore electricity infrastructure. This leads to a wide spectrum of legal issues including the applicability of national laws to infrastructure in the North Sea, the geographical scope of application of support schemes for renewable energy and a lack of harmonisation of national legislation, for instance regarding grid connection regimes.

Regulatory issues are especially contentious because they bear the potential of adversely affecting investor decisions. Because the operation of transmission infrastructure is a natural monopoly, infrastructure operators are subjected to legal provisions that aim to prevent any abuse of their dominant position. Furthermore, they have to observe public service obligations requiring them to safeguard security of supply and promote renewable energy. However, the law attaches different obligations to different kinds of infrastructure operators.

1. Types of infrastructure

The EU and national legal frameworks for electricity infrastructure provide different definitions for different kinds of electricity transmission infrastructure. Only one of them is laid out in the EU law and can thus be considered harmonised. It is the definition of the term 'interconnector', which can be found in Article 2 of the Regulation on Cross-Border Trade for Electricity. The provision states that an interconnector is "a transmission line which crosses or spans a border between Member States and which connects the national transmission system of the Member States".

Other infrastructure types that are frequently used in EU or national legislation, e.g. electricity line, transmission line, grid or electricity network, are only defined in national laws, if they are defined at all. Where they exist, the definitions vary. However, in most cases there is some kind of common understanding on the basis of technical facts. A connection line, for instance, is generally considered to be a transmission line which connects an offshore wind farm to a national transmission system.

With an increasing interconnection of offshore infrastructure it will likely become more and more difficult to differentiate the different types of infrastructure. It is hardly possible to apply the existing definitions to the new kind

13 *Säcker/König/Scholz*, Der regulierungsrechtliche Rahmen für ein Offshore-Stromnetz in der Nordsee, (P. Lang, 2014), p. 41 ff.

of infrastructure that is evolving in the North Sea. It is particularly difficult to distinguish interconnectors from connection lines. The main reason is that the North Sea does not belong to the North Sea coastal States' territories. According to Articles 2(1) and 3(1) of the United Nations Convention on the Law of the Sea (UNCLOS), the territorial sea that defines the maritime border of a State must not exceed 12 nautical miles measured from the baseline. Thus, most of the North Sea is 'a space beyond borders', which makes it difficult to apply the 'cross-border' part of the interconnector definition cited above. In a way, the whole offshore grid can be considered as crossing a border between Member States and connecting their national transmission systems.

Figure 3: Identification of infrastructure types.

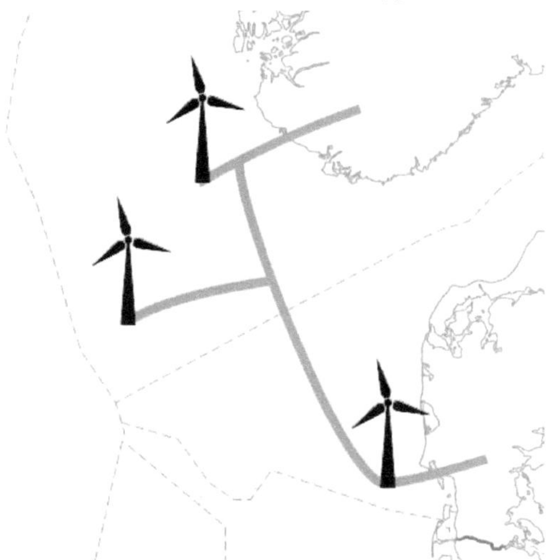

The difficulties arising from the 'beyond border status' of the North Sea can be illustrated with the figure above. Which part of the pictured infrastructure system – that does not exist today, but exemplifies what might evolve in the future – meets the interconnector definition of the Regulation on Cross-Border Trade for Electricity? Where exactly does the interconnector begin, and where exactly does it end? What part of the system can be defined as a connection line connecting an offshore wind farm to a national transmission system? Can the whole infrastructure be defined as both an interconnector and a connection cable?

The fact that it is difficult to apply the existing infrastructure definitions to what is currently evolving in the North Sea is challenging from a legal point of view.[14] As already mentioned, both the EU and national legal frameworks attach different obligations to different kinds of infrastructure operators.

Thus, if it is unclear how to categorize a certain infrastructure it will be difficult to identify the obligations its operator has to meet. Furthermore, a conflict of application of law arises where a certain infrastructure can be categorized as meeting the requirements of more than one infrastructure definition. A particularly interesting conflict shall be demonstrated hereinafter in greater detail: the contradictory obligations following from the European regulatory regime for the promotion of renewable energies and the European regulatory regime for interconnectors.

2. RES Directive

Article 16(2) of the RES Directive stipulates a priority or guaranteed access for electricity produced from renewable energies. More specifically, Article 16(2) (b) of the RES Directive determines a priority access or guaranteed access to "the grid-system", and Article 16(2) (c) of the Directive states that "when dispatching electricity generating installations, transmission system operators shall give priority to generating installations using renewable energy sources". Already today, these provisions also apply to interconnectors although their narrow wording may indicate otherwise.[15] This follows primarily from the purpose of Article 16(2) of the RES Directive.

The provision is not restricted to certain types of infrastructure; hence, it is plausible that the priority access was intended to be universal. By this means, electricity from renewable sources can be promoted in the most effective way, which satisfies the main purpose of the Directive. Furthermore, Article 16(2) of the RES Directive is *lex specialis* to Article 32 of the Electricity Market Directive on third party access.

Thus, since Article 32 of the Electricity Market Directive is applicable to interconnectors, which explicitly follows from Article 17(1) of the Regulation on Cross-Border Trade for Electricity, it is only logical to apply Article 16(2) of the RES Directive to interconnectors as well.

Although this interpretation of Article 16(2) of the RES Directive has not yet been tested in practice, investors already seem to rely on it. The transmission

14 *Säcker/König/Scholz*, Der regulierungsrechtliche Rahmen für ein Offshore-Stromnetz in der Nordsee, (P. Lang, 2014), p. 41 ff.

15 *König*, Engpassmanagement in der deutschen und europäischen Elektrizitätsversorgung, (Nomos, 2013), p. 202 ff.

system operators 50Hertz, TenneT and Energinet.dk are currently exploring how transmission infrastructure can be used both as an interconnector *and* for transporting electricity generated in offshore wind farms. One relevant project in this context, the *Cobra Cable*, has already been mentioned above. If it proves technically feasible to directly connect offshore wind farms to the cable, TenneT and Energinet.dk seek to use its capacity primarily for the transmission of electricity from offshore wind farms. Only if there is not enough electricity generated to use the whole capacity, it is to be used instead of cross-border exchanges in electricity. Similar plans exist for *Kriegers Flak*, a joint project of 50Hertz and Energinet.dk in the Baltic Sea.

At a later stage of this project, which will consist of several offshore wind farms, the transmission system operators seek to build an interconnector between one wind farm in the German and another in the Danish exclusive economic zone, i.e. they plan to implement what has been introduced above as a hub-to-hub connection. Thus, the connection cables of both wind farms could be used for cross-border exchanges in electricity whenever they are not needed for transporting electricity from offshore generation. Similar to the *Cobra Cable*, it is planned to use this interconnector primarily for transporting electricity from offshore wind farms, i.e. to implement a priority access for electricity from renewable sources.

It is, however, highly questionable if EU law allows to use interconnectors primarily for transporting electricity from offshore generation. Although this way of managing capacities is covered by the stipulation of a priority or guaranteed access for electricity from renewable sources in Article 16(2) of the RES Directive, legal certainty is far from assured.

On the contrary, EU law contains a number of provisions specifically addressing the use of interconnector capacities that have to be taken into account as well. As a matter of fact, these provisions hardly leave any room for implementing a priority or guaranteed access to interconnectors for electricity generated from renewable sources.

3. Interconnector regulation

The regulatory regime for interconnectors is laid down in the Regulation on Cross-Border Trade for Electricity, the so called Congestion Management Guidelines, and the Network Code on Capacity Allocation and Congestion Management, which will very likely be the most important framework in practice.

The Network Code was drafted by ENTSO-E according to Article 8 of Regulation on Cross-Border Trade for Electricity and is currently running through the EU's comitology process. It is not yet clear when the Network Code will be entering into force, but it will probably be no later than by the end of 2015. Under the Network Code, the transmission capacity of the interconnectors in the EU will be allocated exclusively by a process called "Market Coupling", which is essentially relying on implicit auctions.[16] Implicit auctions are based on the idea that capacity of interconnectors can be allocated most efficiently if all market figures of the national electricity wholesale markets are already known. Therefore, the Market Coupling mechanism is operated by a central planer called the Market Coupling operator. The Market Coupling operator is provided with two kinds of information: The power exchanges, on the one hand, deliver all necessary information from their order books, including offers and bids, prices and quantities.

The transmission system operators, on the other hand, deliver all necessary information regarding the capacity of interconnectors that is available for cross-border trade in the respective timeframe.

Figure 4: The Market Coupling Mechanism.

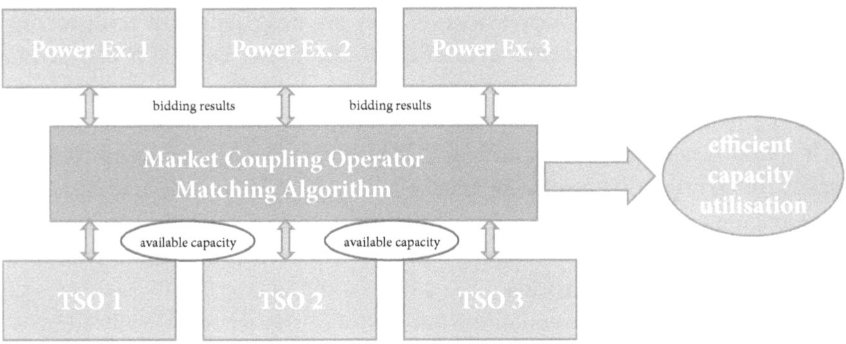

Market Coupling is a way to efficiently allocate scarce transmission capacities, thus, it is a method of congestion management. The general principles of congestion management are laid down in Article 16 of the Regulation on Cross-Border Trade for Electricity. According to Article 16(3) of this Regulation, "[t]he maximum capacity of the interconnections and/or the transmission networks affecting cross-border flows shall be made available to market participants, complying with safety standards of secure network operation". The calculation and allocation of this capacity are described in the Network Code on Capacity Allocation

16 *König*, Engpassmanagement in der deutschen und europäischen Elektrizitätsversorgung, (Nomos, 2013), p. 294 ff.

and Congestion Management in greater detail.[17] EU law, thereby, ensures that the whole available capacity is to be used for cross-border exchanges in electricity.

While strict rules on capacity calculation and allocation are without doubt highly beneficial for cross-border trade and competition, on the one hand, they clearly limit the transmission system operators' ability to use interconnector capacity for other purposes, on the other. Market Coupling rules do not provide for any exemptions regarding the usage of interconnector capacities, i.e. all capacities must be provided to the Market Coupling mechanism.

It is important to know that the Market Coupling rules do not stipulate any kind of priority for electricity from renewable energies. Thus, the Market Coupling regime does not allow for capacity reservations for the benefit of electricity generated from renewable sources. The interconnector operators must notify the whole capacity of their interconnectors to the Market Coupling operator. Neither is the source of electricity taken into account by the Market Coupling operator in the matching process of the Market Coupling algorithm. Thus, the Market Coupling regime as it is set out in the latest draft of the Network Code on Capacity Allocation and Congestion Management leaves no room to grant priority access to offshore wind farms directly connected to an interconnector.

The fact that the Market Coupling rules are so strict in this regard could prove as a significant barrier to all existing plans for tee-in connections, and even hub-to-hub connections. Potential investors may be deterred since, because of the described conflict, it is uncertain if they can implement their ideas for 'double purpose infrastructure' in practice. Indeed, in recent times, Energinet.dk and TenneT have commented only reluctantly on their plans to directly connect offshore wind farms to the *Cobra Cable*. On their websites, both transmission system operators explain that additional efforts are necessary to explore if the tee-in approach is feasible.[18]

---

17 Preliminary service-level draft by DG Energy for a Commission Regulation Establishing a Guideline on Capacity Allocation and Congestion Management, Articles 19 ff.

18 Energinet.dk, Cable to the Netherlands – COBRAcable, http://www.energinet.dk/EN/ANLAEG-OG-PROJEKTER/Anlaegsprojekter-el/Kabel-til-Holland-COBRA/Sider/Kabel-til-Holland-COBRA.aspx (last visited 11/18/2014): "*It is our aim that the connection is based on a new rectifier technology called voltage source converter (VSC) offering the possibility of connecting new offshore wind farms to the cable. COBRAcable could as such become the first step on the road towards establishing a transmission grid in the North Sea capable of supporting wind power expansion and strengthening the European transmission grid.*" Tennet, COBRAcable, http://www.tennet.eu/nl/grid-projects/international-projects/cobracable.html (last visited 11/182014: "*The COBRAcable*

Figure 5: How is it going to work?

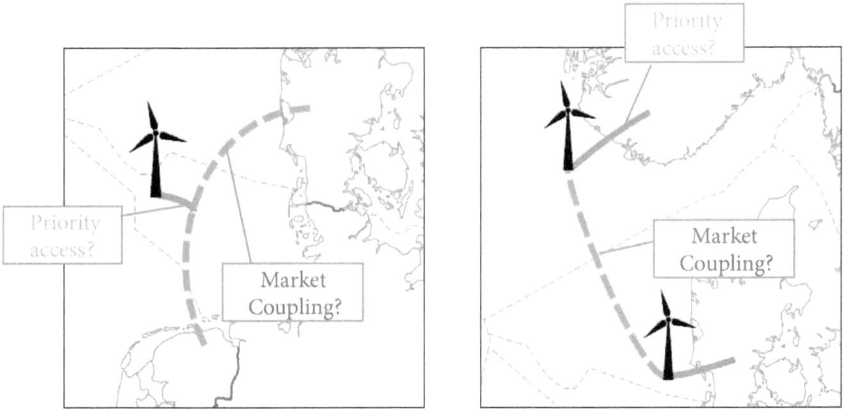

The figure above illustrates the problem. The tee-in connection in the left picture represents what is planned for the Cobra Cable. If the dashed line was considered an interconnector, its capacity would be subject to the Market Coupling mechanism. Thus, it would be impossible to grant priority access to the wind farm directly connected to the interconnector. Clearly, this would make it very difficult for an investor to invest in the wind farm since it was not guaranteed that the electricity generated there could actually be fed into the electricity grid. The right picture represents a hypothetical hub-to-hub connection. This is less problematic compared to the tee-in connection because priority or guaranteed access could be granted to the continuous lines without restriction. However, the availability of the dashed line for cross border trading would be dependent on the dispatching of electricity generated in the adjacent wind farms. If the connection lines were congested with electricity from offshore wind farms, the interconnector could not be used at all for cross-border trading.

In conclusion, the future legal framework for interconnector capacity allocation and congestion management may prove impedimental to the development of an integrated offshore grid in the North Sea for the following reasons:

- Article 16 of the Regulation on Cross-Border Trade for Electricity, the Congestion Management Guidelines and the Network Code for Capacity Allocation

is unique in that it also incorporates the possibility of connecting offshore wind farms to the cable. However additional technical development efforts have to be made before it can be determined whether the use of the new technology needed for this purpose is feasible."

and Congestion Management are *legi speciali* to Article 16 of the RES Directive as regards the use of interconnector capacity;

- These EU rules on capacity allocation and congestion management set up what is called the Market Coupling regime, requiring interconnector operators to notify all available capacities to the Market Coupling mechanism;
- The Market Coupling regime does not allow the implementation of a priority or guaranteed access to interconnectors for electricity generated from renewable sources;
- Under the current legal framework, it is therefore not admissible to use interconnectors primarily for transmitting electricity generated in offshore wind farms.

4. Amending the legal framework

In order to overcome these barriers for the development of an integrated offshore grid in the North Sea, it should be discussed if an amendment to the existing legal framework for interconnector regulation might be feasible. The easiest way would be to include an exemption into the Network Code on Capacity Allocation and Congestion Management that would alleviate the strict requirements for congestion management regarding interconnectors. In an additional provision interconnector operators could be exempted from the obligation to allocate all available interconnector capacities to Market Coupling, as they seek to use them for transmitting electricity generated from offshore wind energy.

More specifically, interconnector operators could be allowed to hold back capacities from the Market Coupling mechanism in order to use them exclusively for the transmission of electricity generated by offshore wind farms. Thus, the capacities would not be available to the market at all. Alternatively, interconnector operators could sell priority transmission rights to offshore wind farm operators, which would grant them the right to be treated preferentially in the Market Coupling algorithm. The latter approach could prove advantageous where there is no feed-in tariff but a direct marketing of electricity by wind farm operators. In any case, it is important to ensure that the preferential treatment for offshore wind farm operators does not endanger the Market Coupling mechanism which is of utmost importance for the completion of the EU's internal electricity market.

Even if the Market Coupling rules were loosened, the provisions on capacity allocation and congestion management could still apply whenever interconnector capacity is not needed to transmit electricity from offshore wind energy, as, for example, when there are no strong winds. Thus, it would still be possible to use the relevant interconnectors for cross-border exchanges in electricity during a significant amount of time. However, amending the legal framework will only be justified if studies show that tee-in connections are technically and economically feasible. Furthermore, the EU legislator should evaluate thoroughly if such amendments are actually fit to fulfil their purpose. Prioritising electricity generated from offshore wind energy may be necessary to ensure that wind farm operators are willing to invest. On the other hand, it must be considered that interconnectors play a significant role for cross-border trade in electricity and thereby contribute to the completion of the internal electricity market. Thus, the two possible functions of interconnectors – transmitting electricity generated from wind energy and fostering cross-border exchanges in electricity – have to be balanced carefully in each individual case.

As an alternative to changing the Market Coupling regime, it should be discussed if it could be feasible to amend only the interconnector definition in Article 2 of the Regulation on Cross-Border Trade for Electricity. The definition could be narrowed down to take into account what was described above as the 'beyond border status' of the North Sea. For the purposes of the Regulation on Cross-Border Trade for Electricity it could be wise to rely on the boundary lines between exclusive economic zones rather than on the actual maritime borders close to the coastlines. Thus, instead of considering the whole electricity infrastructure in the North Sea as "crossing a border between Member States", as Article 2 of the Regulation on Cross-Border Trade for Electricity puts it, only subsea cables crossing a boundary line between two exclusive economic zones could be considered an interconnector. Thus, it would be possible to reduce the scope of application of the Regulation on Cross-Border Trade for Electricity and the Market Coupling regime.

Figure 6: Narrow interconnector definition.

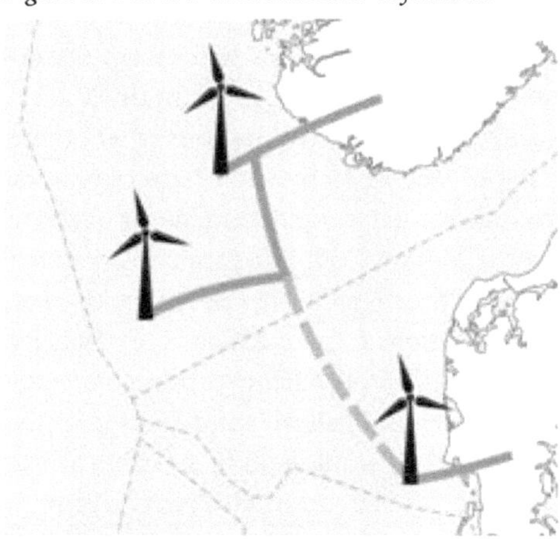

The continuous lines in the figure above would be considered as part of the national grid systems (of Norway and Denmark, respectively). Thus, the offshore grid would be treated in the same way as the onshore grid, i.e. the Regulation on Cross-Border Trade for Electricity and the Market Coupling regime would not apply. Only the subsea cable between the last two nodes on each side of the boundary line between the adjacent exclusive economic zones would be considered as an interconnector and hence be subjected to Market Coupling rules. However, in the long run this option may lead to difficulties if the degree of interconnection is incrementally increased and further wind farms are connected to what has so far been considered as the interconnector. In this case, the interconnector would be 'shortened' in hindsight, and the legal situation would change as well. This could lead to significant planning and investment risks, particularly for the interconnector operator. Nevertheless, this approach could prove advantageous because it basically mirrors the regulatory framework for onshore grids. Thus, it would require only minor amendments to EU energy law.

IV. Conclusion

Electricity infrastructure in the North Sea is quickly evolving. However, the current EU law does not contain provisions on the construction and expansion of offshore grid infrastructure and generation of electricity from offshore wind energy. In many cases, it can be difficult to apply onshore regulations to offshore infrastructure as it has been demonstrated above for the Regulation on Cross-Border Trade for Electricity and the Market Coupling regime.

If the North Sea coastal States want to go forward with their ambitious plans for an offshore electricity grid, amendments to the current legal framework will probably be inevitable. Clearly, this is a big challenge since changing the EU energy law has always been controversial in the past.

The development of an integrated offshore grid requires enormous efforts on both the technical and the regulatory level. However, integrating offshore electricity infrastructure in the North Sea would significantly assist the EU in meeting its energy policy goals. It would contribute to the completion of the EU's internal electricity market and benefit both the integration of wind energy into the electrical system and security of supply. Thus, governments, regulatory authorities and companies should work together to implement the necessary legal framework and ensure an efficient and economic development of the North Sea offshore grid. This would not only benefit the North Sea coastal States, but could as well be imitated by other regions like the Baltic Sea. After all, accessing Europe's vast offshore wind resources will be pivotal for the EU's success in rebuilding its energy industry.

Seminar Conclusions

The contributions in this publication have underlined the impact of the new EU Commission guidelines on State aid for environmental protection and energy on the promotion of renewable energies. In addition, Articles 30 and 110 TFEU as limitations to Member States' renewable energy promotion were assessed with an aim of clarifying the definition of State resources. More importantly, State aid law and the free movement of goods interact. The dialogue between the principle of free movement of goods and national renewable support schemes has triggered a profound legal academic debate. The blurred line between indistinctly and distinctly applicable measures still needs to be clarified by the European Court of Justice.

Renewable energy promotion further requires considerable investments. It is the character of renewable energy disputes in the European Union that has been the focus of attention in this volume. In addition to the priority or guaranteed access regimes stipulated by the RES Directive, renewable energies have entered a heavily regulated area where all investment depends on State policies, State support and the regulatory framework.

In addition, EU renewable energy promotion ultimately depends on and is defined by the competences allocated to the Union by the Member States. Therefore, Article 192 and 194 TFEU cannot be left out of the overall analysis as they are crucial EU primary law provisions. The analysis of their interaction as well as the actual place of renewable energy promotion in the European legal landscape has been described light of a predominant environmental purpose. Lastly, in order to complete the European energy policy triangle, energy security concerns were addressed by explaining how congestion management rules challenge the development of an integrated offshore electricity infrastructure in the North Sea.

Understanding the broader context of EU law within the area of European renewable energy promotion requires legal scholars to identify the actual and potential interaction between several areas of EU law. The current developments and challenges should be observed and discussed by applying the entire spectrum of EU law on the basis of a horizontal reading of the Treaties. The present seminar publication therefore aims to inspire and motivate further academic work on the topics presented. This volume addressed current developments and challenges in

EU renewable energy law by analysing the interaction between different Treaty provisions as well as the implication of EU law on national support systems and investments. The contributions made and the topics discussed at the seminar are not only relevant to renewable energy promotion but also timely and with regards to the current evolution in EU law.

Lydia Scholz
Thea Sveen

Veröffentlichungen des Instituts für deutsches und europäisches Wirtschafts-, Wettbewerbs- und Regulierungsrecht der Freien Universität Berlin

Herausgegeben von Franz Jürgen Säcker

Band 1 Franz Jürgen Säcker (Hrsg.): Deutsch-russisches Energie- und Bergrecht im Vergleich. Ergebnisse einer Arbeitstagung vom 31. März / 1. April 2006. 2007.

Band 2 Franz Jürgen Säcker / Walther Busse von Colbe (Hrsg.): Wettbewerbsfördernde Anreizregulierung. Zum Anreizregulierungsbericht der Bundesnetzagentur vom 30. Juni 2006. 2007.

Band 3 Dirk Zschenderlein: Die Gleichbehandlung der Aktionäre bei der Auskunftserteilung in der Aktiengesellschaft. Zum Problem der Zulässigkeit der Weitergabe von Informationen an einzelne Aktionäre und Dritte. 2007.

Band 4 Simone Kirchhain: Die Anwendung der Vertikal-GVO auf innerstaatliche Wettbewerbsbeschränkungen nach der 7. GWB-Novelle. 2007.

Band 5 Franz Jürgen Säcker: Der Independent System Operator. Ein neues institutionelles Design für Netzbetreiber? 2007.

Band 6 Stefanie Otto: Allgemeininteressen im neuen UWG. § 1 S. 2 UWG und die wettbewerbsfunktionale Auslegung. 2007.

Band 7 Jochen Eichler: Vertragliche Dritthaftung. Eine Auseinandersetzung mit der Frage der Dritthaftung von sogenannten Experten und anderen Auskunftspersonen im Rahmen des § 311 Abs. 3 BGB. 2007.

Band 8 Markela Stamati: Die Anforderungen der operationellen Entflechtung nach den Beschleunigungsrichtlinien der Europäischen Kommission. Umsetzung in Deutschland und Griechenland. 2008.

Band 9 Franz Jürgen Säcker: The Concept of the Relevant Product Market. Between Demand-Side Substitutability and Supply-Side -Substitutability in Competition Law. 2008.

Band 10 Renate Rabensdorf: Die Durchgriffshaftung im deutschen und russischen Recht der Kapitalgesellschaften. Eine rechtsvergleichende Untersuchung. 2009.

Band 11 Franz Jürgen Säcker: Der beschleunigte Ausbau der Höchstspannungsnetze als Rechtsproblem. Erläutert am Beispiel der 380-kV-Höchstspannungsleitung Lauchstädt – Redwitz – Grafenrheinfeld mit Querung des Rennsteigs im Naturpark Thüringer Wald. 2009.

Band 12 Helen Mahne: Eigentum an Versorgungsleitungen. 2009.

Band 13 Franz Jürgen Säcker (Hrsg.): Russisches Energierecht - Gesetzessammlung. 2009.

Band 14 Franz Jürgen Säcker / Maik Wolf: Integrierte Energieversorgung in geschlossenen Verteilernetzen. Zum Gestaltungsspielraum des Gesetzgebers zur Neuregelung des § 110 EnWG im Lichte des Dritten EG-Energiepakets. 2009.

Band 15 Franz Jürgen Säcker (Hrsg.): Das Dritte Energiepaket für den Gasbereich. Deutsch-Englische Textausgabe mit einer Einführung. 2009.

Band 16 Franz Jürgen Säcker (Hrsg.): Das Dritte Energiepaket für den Elektrizitätsbereich. Deutsch-Englische Textausgabe mit einer Einführung. 2009.

Band 17 Thomas Dörmer: Die Unternehmenspacht. Rechtsstellung der Vertragsparteien unter besonderer Berücksichtigung der Pflicht des Unternehmenspächters zur ordnungsgemäßen Unternehmensführung sowie der Rechtslage bei Vertragsbeendigung. 2010.

Band 18 Klaas Bosch: Die Kontrolldichte der gerichtlichen Überprüfung von Marktregulierungsentscheidungen der Bundesnetzagentur nach dem Telekommunikationsgesetz. 2010.

Band 19 Geng-Sook Leem: Einheitliche Corporate Governance-Grundsätze für die Europäische Aktiengesellschaft (SE). Eine rechtsvergleichende Untersuchung anhand der Ausgestaltung der SE im deutschen und britischen Recht. 2010.

Band 20 Wiebke Gebhardt: Gentechnik und Koexistenz nach der Gesetzesnovelle von 2008: Zivilrechtliche Haftung im Vergleich Deutschland und USA. 2010.

Band 21 Cathrin Isenberg: Die Geruchsmarke als Gemeinschaftsmarke. Schutzfähigkeit und Einsatzmöglichkeiten. 2010.

Band 22 Franz Jürgen Säcker / Jochen Mohr / Maik Wolf: Konzessionsverträge im System des europäischen und deutschen Wettbewerbsrechts. 2011.

Band 23 Judith Antonia Loeck: Die unzumutbare Belästigung nach der UWG Novelle 2008 und dem Gesetz zur Bekämpfung unerlaubter Telefonwerbung und zur Verbesserung des Verbraucherschutzes bei besonderen Betriebsformen. 2011.

Band 24 Jörg Jaecks: Konzernverrechnungsklauseln und verwandte einseitige Verrechnungsbefugnisse im Mehrpersonenverhältnis. 2011.

Band 25 Franz Jürgen Säcker: Marktabgrenzung, Marktbeherrschung, Markttransparenz und Machtmissbrauch auf den Großhandelsmärkten für Elektrizität. 2011.

Band 26 Susanne Wende: Die einheitliche Auslegung von Beihilfen- und Vergaberecht als Teilgebiete des europäischen Wettbewerbsrechts. 2011.

Band 27 Leonie Kempel: Die Anwendung von Art. 102 AEUV auf geistiges Eigentum und Sacheigentum. Die Voraussetzungen des Kontrahierungszwangs nach Art. 102 AEUV und der Essential-Facility-Doktrin unter besonderer Berücksichtigung der Unterschiede zwischen geistigem Eigentum und Sacheigentum. 2011.

Band 28 Christoph Schuldt: Werbejingles – schützenswerte Kompositionen!? Die urheberrechtliche und markenrechtliche Schutzfähigkeit von Werbejingles vor unbefugter Nachahmung. 2012.

Band 29 Lydia Scholz: Die Rechtfertigung von diskriminierenden umweltpolitischen Steuerungsinstrumenten. Eine Untersuchung der Reichweite der Warenverkehrsfreiheit und ihrer Begrenzung durch den Umweltschutz als Vertragsziel am Beispiel der deutschen Energiefördergesetze EEG und KWKModG. 2012.

Band 30 Franz Jürgen Säcker: Investitionen in Kraftwerke zur Sicherung einer zuverlässigen Elektrizitätsversorgung nach der Energiewende. Rechtliche und ökonomische Rahmenbedingungen. 2012.

Band 31 Florian Leib: Kartellrechtliche Durchsetzungsstrategien in der Europäischen Union, den USA und Deutschland. Eine rechtsvergleichende Darstellung. 2012.

Band 32 Holger Hoch: Marktverschlusseffekte und Effizienzen vertikaler Zusammenschlüsse. Kartellrechtliche Beurteilung nach europäischem und deutschem Recht. 2012.

Band 33 Sebastian Kemper: Gasnetzzugang in Deutschland und in Spanien. 2012.

Band 34 Elena Timofeeva: Unbundling in der russischen Elektrizitätswirtschaft im Vergleich zum deutschen und europäischen Energierecht. 2012.

Band 35 Gisela Drozella / Harald Krebs: Marktbeherrschung im Bereich Stromerzeugung / Stromgroßhandel. Eine kritische Analyse der neueren Sicht des Bundeskartellamts. 2013.

Band 36 Christian Rehm: Die Einzel- und Gesamtverantwortung der Vorstandsmitglieder der Aktiengesellschaft. Die Verantwortung für die Leitung und Geschäftsführung im mehrköpfigen Vorstand in der unabhängigen und der herrschenden AG. 2013.

Band 37 Ann-Christin Richter: Mengen- und umsatzbezogene Rabatte marktbeherrschender Unternehmen in den Grenzen des Art. 102 AEUV. 2013.

Band 38 Nikolaos Pitsos: Die erhebliche Behinderung des wirksamen Wettbewerbs (SIEC-Test) im Fusionskontrollrecht. Zugleich ein Beitrag zur Problematik der oligopolistischen Marktbeherrschung unter Vergleich mit dem amerikanischen SLC-Test. 2013.

Band 39 Mirko Heinemann: Das Markenzeichen als Anknüpfungspunkt des Markenimages. 2013.

Band 40 Sylvia Lorenz: Der Immaterialgüterschutz virtueller Ladengeschäfte. Ein Vorschlag für die rechtliche Erfassung virtueller Güter. 2014.

Band 41 Anke Reimers: Wettbewerbsrechtliche und regulatorische Analyse der Kapazitätenvergabe an Grenzkuppelstellen im Elektrizitätsbinnenmarkt. 2014.

Band 42 Franz Jürgen Säcker / Carsten König / Lydia Scholz: Der regulierungsrechtliche Rahmen für ein Offshore-Stromnetz in der Nordsee. 2014.

Band 43 David Preisendanz: Der Humor in der vergleichenden Werbung. 2014.

Band 44 Martin Gerig: Vollendung des EU-Energiebinnenmarktes vs. nationale Marktabschottungen. Europarechtskonformität mitgliedstaatlicher Fördermaßnahmen und Kapazitätsmärkte am Beispiel Deutschlands. 2014.

Band 45 Jan Patrick Ehinger: Dritthaftung für Kunstexpertisen und Aufnahmebestätigungen in den Catalogue raisonné. Ein Beitrag zur Expertenhaftung. 2014.

Band 46 Julia Gerzen: Das Recht der Gesellschafter-Fremdkapitalfinanzierung. Rechtsvergleichende Analyse der Behandlung von Gesellschafterdarlehen vor und in der Insolvenz der GmbH nach deutschem und russischem Recht. 2014.

Band 47 Laura Börger: Die gerichtliche Kontrolldichte bei der Überprüfung von Entscheidungen der Europäischen Kommission auf dem Gebiet der Fusionskontrolle. 2014.

Veröffentlichungen des Instituts für Energie- und Regulierungsrecht Berlin

Band 48 Daniel Simon Travers: Kopplungsangebote. Eine Studie zum Vertrags- und Lauterkeitsrecht. 2015.

Band 49 Anna Olbryś-Sobieszuk: EU-rechtliche Schranken der Glücksspielwerbung in Deutschland, Großbritannien und Polen. 2015.

Band 50 Franz Jürgen Säcker/Lydia Scholz/Thea Sveen: Renewable Energy Law in Europe. Challenges and Perspectives. 2015.

Band 51 Lina Berezgova: Festlegung von Stromnetzentgelten in Deutschland und Russland. Eine rechtsvergleichende Untersuchung der anreizbasierten Regulierungsvorgaben. 2015.

Band 52 Fengliang Jin: Aufgreifkriterien in der Fusionskontrolle. Eine rechtsvergleichende Untersuchung des europäischen (Art. 3 FKVO), deutschen (§ 37 GWB), taiwanesischen (§ 6 FHG) und festlandchinesischen (§ 20 AMG) Rechts. 2015.

Band 53 Vasileios Triantafyllidis: Die Einordnung der Passing-On-Defense in das allgemeine Schadensersatzrecht. Eine rechtsvergleichende, dogmatische Studie. 2015.

www.ingramcontent.com/pod-product-compliance
Ingram Content Group UK Ltd.
Pitfield, Milton Keynes, MK11 3LW, UK
UKHW041826031026
15587UKWH00002B/599

9 783631 663431